Future Men

Titles in the Family Series:

Reforming Marriage

Her Hand in Marriage
Biblical Courtship in the Modern World

Standing on the Promises
A Handbook on Biblical Childrearing

The Fruit of Her Hands
Respect and the Christian Woman

Federal Husband

Fidelity
What It Means to Be a One-Woman Man

Praise Her in the Gates
The Calling of Christian Motherhood

Future Men
Raising Boys to Fight Giants

My Life for Yours
A Walk through the Christian Home

Visit www.canonpress.com for more details.

Future Men

Raising Boys to Fight Giants

DOUGLAS WILSON

canonpress
Moscow, Idaho

Published by Canon Press
P.O. Box 8729, Moscow, ID 83843
800.488.2034 | www.canonpress.com

Printed in the United States of America.
Cover design by Rachel Hoffman.
Cover art: La Lutte (wrestling), Emile Friant, 1889
Used with permission of the Art Renewal Center, Port Reading,
New Jersey: www. artrenewal.org

11 12 13 14 15 16 17   16 15 14 13 12

This book is dedicated to Heather,
who has blessed us by marrying the man
who was once our future man.

Contents

Introduction. 9

Understanding Future Men
1. The Shape of Masculinity 13
2. Effeminacy and Biblical Masculinity 19

Molding Future Men
3. A Call for Fathers 27
4. A Covenant Home. 35
5. Doctrinal Meat. 43

Future Men Against Themselves
6. Secret Sin, Tolerated Sin 53
7. Laziness and Hard Labor 59
8. Money Paths and Traps. 67
9. Christian Liberty 75

Future Men with Others
10. Mom and Sisters. 83
11. Church and Worship 93
12. Giants, Dragons, and Books. 101
13. School Work. 109
14. Friends 117
15. Fighting, Sports, and Competition 125
16. Girls and Sex. 135
17. Courtship and Betrothal 145
18. Contempt for the Cool 153

Conclusion: Fighting Idols 165

Appendix A: Liberty and Marijuana. 173
Appendix B: Proverbs Was Written for Boys. 185
Acknowledgments 193
Index of Scripture. 195

Introduction

As much as it may distress us, our boys are future men. I was once leading a seminar for teachers at our Christian school, and in the course of the discussion mentioned that many of the girls in the school would, within a few short years, be adult women and would take their place in our midst. The teachers heard all this with aplomb, but when I went on to say that within a few short years the *boys* they were instructing would be lawyers, airline pilots, pastors, etc., the looks on the faces of the assembled teachers ranged from concern to mild panic. Boys take a lot of faith.

This is good because the presence or absence of faith reveals whether or not we have a biblical doctrine of our future. Unbelief is always anchored to the present, while faith looks at that which is unseen. But even here we only get half the picture. Too often we think that faith only looks at unseen *heavenly* things, but this truncated approach is really the result of an incipient gnosticism. In the Bible, faith includes the ability to see that which is unseen because it is still future. Abraham rejoiced to see the day of Christ, not the day when he, Abraham, would go to heaven. Faith conquers kingdoms, faith stops the mouths of lions, faith turns armies to flight, and faith brings boys up to a mature and godly masculinity.

But another qualification must be added. The faith exhibited by wise parents of boys is the faith of a farmer, or a sculptor, or anyone else engaged in the work of shaping unfolding possibilities. It is not the faith of someone waiting around for lightening to strike; it is the faith of someone who looks at the present and sees what it will become—through grace and good works.

Countless examples may be multiplied from any given day in the life of a small boy. Say a boy breaks a chair because he was jumping on it from the bunk bed. Unbelief sees the cost of replacing the chair. Faith sees aggressiveness and courage, both of which obviously need to be directed and disciplined. Suppose a boy gets into a fight protecting his sister. Unbelief sees the lack of wisdom that created a situation that could have been easily avoided; faith sees an immature masculinity that is starting to assume the burden of manhood.

Unbelief squashes; faith *teaches* while it directs. Faith takes a boy aside, and tells him that this part of what he did was good, while that other part of what he did got in the way. "And this is how to do it better next time."

This issue of fighting provides a good example of how necessary such distinctions are. Of course parents do not want to encourage their sons to pick fights with other boys. But this is not the only item on the menu. Neither do they want to encourage abdication and cowardice. There are times when men have to fight. It follows that there will be times when boys have to *learn* how to fight, how to walk away, how to turn the other cheek, when to turn the other cheek, and when to put up their dukes. If boys don't learn, men won't know. And boys will not learn unless their fathers teach.

When Theodore Roosevelt was at Harvard, he taught Sunday school for a time at Christ Church, until he was dismissed over an issue related to this. A boy showed up one Sunday with a black eye. He admitted he had been fighting, and on a Sunday too. He told the future president that a bigger boy had been pinching his sister, and so he fought him. TR told him that he had done perfectly right and gave him a dollar. The vestrymen thought this was a bit much, and so they let their exuberant Sunday school teacher go.

Unbelief cannot look past the surface. If there was any sin involved, unbelief sees only the sin. Faith sees what was turned aside to the service of sin and seeks to turn it back again. Sin is parasitic and cannot function without some good attributes that it seeks to corrupt. Consequently, faith must distinguish that which must be preserved and developed and that which must be abandoned because of the sin.

In addition, faith also sees the godliness in what many pietists, on their own authority, have come to *call* sin. At the beginning of his life, a boy does not know what century he was born in, and consequently exhibits to many of his politically correct and aghast elders some of the same traits exhibited by the boyhood chums of Sennacherib and Charlemagne. He doesn't know any better—yet. But in our day, many of these creation-design masculine traits are drilled or drugged out of him by the time he is ten. Faith resists this ungodly process and defines sin by the Scriptures and not by pietistic traditions.

So faith is central in bringing up boys, but it is important to remember that the object of faith is not the *boy*. It is faith in *God*, faith in His promises, faith in His wisdom. Faith *concerns* the boy, and the boy can see that it concerns him. Parents are to believe God *for* their sons, which is a very different thing than believing *in* their sons.

But faith in the wisdom of God cannot be separated from the standard of Scripture. It is easy for us to ask God to give us "faith" to accomplish whatever it is that *we* think is a good idea. But this is not what we are called to do. We are Christians and cannot survive on bread alone. We must live by and on the Word of God.

Because we should want to base the training of our boys on the standards and patterns of Scripture, we may be encouraged to look to the promises of Scripture as well. These promises are not a later "add-on"; they are foundational to the whole process. Faith is not wishful thinking; faith apprehends the promises of God found in Scripture. "The children of thy servants shall continue, and their seed shall be established before thee" (Ps. 102:28). Faith sees a son *as* established, and the work of faith goes on to establish him. Faith is the assurance of things hoped for, the evidence of things not seen.

As we look to the Scriptures for the pattern of masculinity that we are to set before our sons, we will find them manifested perfectly in the life of the Lord Jesus Christ. He is the incarnate Word, the One who embodies perfectly all that Scripture teaches in words. As we look at the teaching of Scripture throughout this book on what it means to be a man (and therefore, what it means to be a future man), we will come back again and again to the example of Jesus Christ. He is the one who set for us the ultimate pattern for friendship, for courage, for faithfulness, and integrity.

God is the one who places a specific boy in a particular home. And He does so in order that those parents who believe and obey Him might come to delight in a wise son, a son who is like Jesus Christ. "My son, if thine heart be wise, my heart shall rejoice, even mine. Yea, my reins shall rejoice, when thy lips speak right things" (Prov. 23:15–16).

With these introductory things said, a few words are necessary about some overlap with material found in some of my other books on the family. The first point is that while repetition may be a headache for editors, it remains a pastoral necessity (Phil. 3:1). We moderns need to internalize many of these truths, and an important part of this is repetition. Secondly, there are times when a point made in an earlier work needs to be expanded or qualified. Sometimes a point made elsewhere is clear to some and murky to others. Third, although there are some hardy devotees of my stuff who will soldier manfully through more than one of my books, this is not the case for everyone. And because of how the books are frequently used (group studies, etc.), the books pretty much need to stand alone. Not everyone reads the earlier books. And last, sometimes I repeat myself because I am getting older and can't help it.

CHAPTER ONE

The Shape of Masculinity

Before taking a road trip, it is a very good idea to have some idea of where you are going. Before rearing a son to be "masculine," it is equally important to have some notion of what that is. For Christians seeking to be biblical, it is important to have that definition of masculinity grounded in the teaching of Scripture.

So what is masculinity? What are we looking for when we describe manhood according to the Bible? The answer to that question will inform and direct all our efforts in bringing up our sons. Manhood is where boyhood should be aimed.

Douglas Jones has helpfully argued that masculinity can be thought of as "the collection of all those characteristics which flow from delighting in and sacrificing bodily strength for goodness." Bill Mouser makes this point even stronger by pointing to the five clear aspects of this kind of masculinity throughout the Bible. As with every such categorization, we cannot make these five aspects watertight, separating them completely from one another, but nevertheless, these *are* distinctive features of the masculine constitution.

Men are created to exercise dominion over the earth; they are fitted to be husbandman, tilling the earth; they are equipped to be saviors, delivering from evil; they are expected to grow up into wisdom, becoming sages; and they are designed to reflect the image and glory of God. Some of these following terms may seem somewhat cumbersome to some, but let's call them *lords, husbandmen, saviors, sages,* and *glory-bearers.*

This chapter will not make a detailed case for these roles but will simply outline and describe the features of each and then show how each one should manifest itself in the life of boys. Of course, when these are neglected, or worse, resisted, the consequences are very harmful to boys.

Lords: Man was created to exercise dominion in the earth. The charge which God gave in this regard is frequently called the cultural mandate.

> And God said, Let us make man in our image, after our likeness: and let them have dominion over the fish of the sea, and over the fowl of the air, and over the cattle, and over all the earth, and over every creeping thing that creepeth upon the earth. . . . Be fruitful, and multiply, and replenish the earth, and subdue it. (Gen. 1:26–28)

Some may assume that this cultural mandate is negated by the fall of man into sin, but God repeats the mandate again after the flood (Gen. 9:1). Sin certainly affected our ability to fulfill this command from God, but it did not remove the obligation placed on us by the command. But if it is to be fulfilled now, in a sinful world, then it must be as a result of the goodness and grace of God. And this is what we see. The mandate is given to us yet again in another form in the Great Commission. We are told there to disciple the nations and bring them to true submission to the Lord Jesus Christ (Mt. 28:18–20).

In boys, we might call this the "tree fort" impetus. Boys want to conquer and subdue, and if the terrain before them is the back yard, then that is what they want to conquer and subdue. The point of discipline with boys is to channel and direct their energy into an obedient response to the cultural mandate. It is not to squash that energy, destroying it or making it sullen. Boys therefore should be in training to become men who exercise dominion; they should be learning to be lords in the earth; they should learn to be *adventurous* and *visionary*.

Husbandmen: Man was created, not only to discover and conquer new worlds, but also to make those worlds flourish. The dominion mandate, taken in isolation, could result in men trying to build a culture based on piracy and freebooting. This second aspect means that men are created to conquer and subdue, and after this, *to settle down*. After man was created, God placed him in the garden to tend and protect it: "the LORD God took the man and put him in the garden of Eden to *tend* and *keep* it" (Gen. 2:15).

Man does not just build bridges and space stations. He must also tend and oversee the organic things which he plants there—gardens, families, towns. Great lessons can be acquired by small boys in a small garden. A rich farmer was once rebuked for having his sons work in the fields when they didn't have to. His reply was apropos to this discussion. He wasn't raising corn, he explained, he was raising boys. Boys therefore should be learning to be *patient, careful,* and *hard-working*.

Saviors: Men also have a deep desire to *deliver* or save. The great example of a savior is, of course, the Lord Jesus Christ. His deliverance was promised to His people in the early chapters of Genesis: "And I will put enmity between thee and the woman, and between thy seed and her seed; it shall bruise thy head, and thou shalt bruise his heel" (Gen. 3:14–15).

The ancient serpent, this dragon, was the tempter who brought the occasion of sin before Adam and Eve. God promised here a curse on the serpent, and in that curse we see the salvation of the world. That salvation cannot be separated from the destruction of the lying worm. As I write this, my two-year-old grandson is learning the story of St. George and the dragon. It absolutely captivates him, and he can't get enough of it. He is learning something profound here. Men who follow Jesus Christ, the dragon-slayer, must themselves become lesser dragon-slayers. And this is why it is absolutely *essential* for boys to play with wooden swords and plastic guns. Boys have a deep need to have something to defend, something to represent in battle. And to beat the spears into pruning hooks prematurely, before the war is over, will leave you fighting the dragon with a pruning hook.

The Christian faith is in no way pacifistic. The peace that will be ushered in by our great Prince will be a peace purchased with blood. As our Lord sacrificed Himself in this war, so must His followers learn to do.

Boys must learn that they are growing up to fight in a great war, and they must consequently learn, as boys, to be *strong, sacrificial, courageous*, and *good*.

Sage: The sage is a man who is great in wisdom, and wisdom in Scripture is personified as a great lady. Sons are exhorted constantly to listen to her. As we look to the first part of Proverbs (1–9), we see that wisdom is a *woman* who disciplines boys. When a grimy little boy needs his knuckles rapped, she is the one to do it. If he heeds wisdom in her role as the strict school-mistress, he grows up to a certain measure of wisdom, and the Lady Wisdom becomes his patroness. And when a man has grown up to wisdom, he has become a sage.

We must therefore teach our boys the masculinity of study, of learning, of books, of intellectual discussion. Too often we let boys drift into a situation where they pit one aspect of masculinity against another. When this happens, for example, a boy who naturally loves the outdoors can too readily dismiss software programming as effeminate, or, even worse, come to look down on poetry. Intellectual discipline, or, as Peter put it, girding up the loins of the mind, is an important part of growing to manhood.

In boyhood, study looks suspiciously like digging a hole and then filling it up. The author of Hebrews tells us that no discipline seems pleasant at the time, but rather painful. *Afterwards*, he says, it yields the peaceful fruit of an upright life. Nowhere is this principle more clear than in the relationship of study in the early years to wisdom in the years of old age. And while the point is clear when we make it this way, it is not naturally visible to a boy who has to do a homework assignment when he can hear all the neighborhood kids playing kick the can. The connections must be made for him. Boys must therefore learn to be *teachable, studious,* and *thoughtful.*

Glory-bearers: The last aspect of masculinity is seen in the fact that men are the glory of God. Paul puts the matter very plainly. "For a man indeed ought not to cover his head, forasmuch as he is the image and glory of God: but the woman is the glory of the man" (1 Cor. 11:7). The woman reflects the glory of God by reflecting the glory of man, whose glory she is. However much modern egalitarians do not like it, God did not make the world according to their specifications. The head of every man is Christ, and the head of every woman is man (1 Cor. 11:3). This teaching on headship is repeated by Paul elsewhere. "For the husband is the head of the wife, even as Christ is the head of the church: and he is the saviour of the body. Therefore as the church is subject unto Christ, so let the wives be to their own husbands in every thing" (Eph. 5:23–24).

These distinctions are not made in the interests of winning a competition. Star differs from star in glory. The sun and the moon differ from one another. When the Bible assigns one kind of glory to man and another kind of glory to woman, our modern egalitarian bigotries prevent us from seeing that they are different kinds and levels of *glory.*

G. K. Chesterton wrote a short poem entitled "Comparisons" that summarizes the problem exactly.

If I set the sun beside the moon,
And if I set the land beside the sea,
And if I set the town beside the country,
And if I set the man beside the woman,
I suppose some fool would talk about one being better.

Because these things are true, boys must be instructed on how to grow up into glory and how to fulfill their responsibility to be *representative, responsible,* and *holy.*

Putting all this together, we should have a pretty good sense of where we are going. We should want our boys to be aggressive and adventurous. They are learning to be lords of the earth. We should want them to be patient and hardworking. They are learning husbandry. We should want them to hate evil and to have a deep desire to fight it. They are learning what a weapon feels like in their hands. We should want boys to be eager to learn from the wise. They are learning to become wise themselves. We should want them to stand before God, in the worship of God, with head uncovered. They are the image and glory of God.

CHAPTER TWO

Effeminacy and Biblical Masculinity

We live in a feminist and effeminate culture. Because of this, at best, as a people we are uneasy with masculinity, and with increasing regularity, whenever it manages to appear somehow, we call for someone to do something about it.

There are two basic directions a boy can take in departing from biblical masculinity. One is the option of effeminacy, and the other is a macho-like counterfeit masculinity. With the former, he takes as a model a set of virtues which are not supposed to be *his* virtues. With the latter, he adopts a set of pseudo-virtues, practices which are not virtues at all.

When God has assigned a place, a station, to someone, it is disobedience to desert that station. A woman is no coward for refusing to desert her children in order to enlist in the army to go off and fight in a war. But a man who refuses to fight can be charged (depending on the circumstances) with cowardice. This same pattern can be seen in all the little things of life. A man is not supposed to stand around when it is important to exercise leadership. A woman might be called to simply wait for her husband to make a decision. But a man who waits around for *someone* to decide is abdicating his assigned role.

Of course a biblical man is to be kind and gentle, but the model for this is to be (ultimately) the Lord Jesus, and in conjunction with this, the teaching of Scripture. The overarching model for this is not our composite cultural picture of what an accommodating male looks like. When distortions occur, they can veer left into effeminacy, or right into a counterfeit masculinity.

Feminine Boys

Because of the egalitarian times we live in, we first have to say a few words in defense of stereotyping. Generalizations, *understood to be such,* are not only permissible but necessary. Jesus speaks about the Pharisees as a class, although there were Pharisees who were not the kind of hypocrites He rightfully castigated. In fact, we can define a good Pharisee as one who acknowledged the justice of His generalization—and then came to Him by night to receive instruction about regeneration. The apostle Paul committed the egalitarian *faux pas* of lumping Cretans together into one large, lazy gluttonous mass. But he still knew there were good Cretans, and he made a point of quoting one of them.

This said, boys should not play with dolls, and boys who do play with them have a problem. One of the themes of this book is to reinforce the truism that the boy is father to the man. What you have young you will have more of later, old.

For most boys, the right general response to effeminacy is natural (as in, *yuck*), but instruction and correction is still necessary. This is because the boys do not know how to make the distinction between that which should be mocked in effeminate boys and that which must be honored in the girls. And for those boys who gravitate toward playing house, and dolls, and dress-ups, wise parental control, oversight, and redirection is necessary.

But in order to do this properly, a right understanding of masculinity (on the part of the parents) is necessary. Small boys tend to think that masculinity consists of rolling around in the dirt, and so they are likely to dismiss a quiet studiousness in a boy as simply another form of indoor effeminacy. But we have already seen that a boy should be studying to become wise, studying to be a sage when he is old. This is not the same thing as wearing a frilly apron. Put another way, the distinction between masculinity and femininity is not one of "outdoors" and "indoors." Women can consider a field and buy it for a vineyard, they can work in the garden, they can tend the fruit trees, and be a glory to their sex. Men can work inside too, helping and leading with many domestic duties, though their focus will be different. Role relationships are clear to the wise, but for those who want life to conform to wooden simplicities, they are a stumbling block.

And this is where the collective wisdom of many generations can help us out—through stereotypes. Far from being a repository of thoughtless bigotries, our stereotypes help us to appreciate a traditional wisdom. When boys learn the rudiments of cooking, as they should, they should also learn to do it in a masculine way. What way is that? To the stereotypes! Boys should learn to glory in being boys, and they should learn to relate all their activities to this. When parents help their boys broaden their scope (getting beyond rolling around in the dirt), this is not so that the distinction between the boys and their sisters can be blurred, but rather so that it might be reinforced *in many other areas.* This should be seen in the kind of books read, the kind of music listened to, the kind of movies watched, the kind of household tasks assigned, the kind of games played, and so forth. The fact that some of the distinctions seem to us arbitrary—why is taking out the garbage manly and using the garbage disposal womanly?— should cause us joy and satisfaction, not confusion. Profound forces are at work. We should let our great, great grandparents teach us something.

One additional caution. Many times fathers who are domineering (as opposed to fathers who exercise a godly leadership) will browbeat their sons into a pattern of cowering submission which is effeminate. They then wonder why their sons do not follow their example, but the reason is that the father would not permit it. He was not training his son; he was sitting on him.

Counterfeit Masculinity

The opposite problem to effeminacy is that of embracing, enthusiastically, a truncated view of masculinity, what I call counterfeit masculinity. This problem "glories" in masculinity, but has a view of it that no wise observer should consider glorious at all. There is more to masculinity than grunting and bluster.

Counterfeit masculinity excels at making excuses. Because the "masculinity" is a matter of pride, not humble acceptance of responsibility, then anything which threatens that pride must be rejected. One of the things which always threatens pride is any kind of failure, and the way that insecure males deal with this is through making excuses. True masculinity accepts responsibility, period, while false masculinity will try to accept responsibility only for success. This is a key distinction and is worth pursuing at some length.

Suppose a young son is playing left field, and in the course of the game, he drops an easy pop fly. Suppose further that he says he did so because "the sun was in my eyes", "a bee was near me," "the grass was slippery," "a fan yelled and distracted me," and so on. This should be taken with the utmost seriousness by the parents—this boy is in grave spiritual danger. This pattern of fending off a threat of wounded pride through excuse-making is typical of males in sin, and yet is *thoroughly* unmasculine. A refusal to make excuses is right at the heart of a scriptural masculinity.

Boys need so much practice at this that they should be taught to accept responsibility even when the sun *was* in their eyes. Unfortunately, many boys are schooled in the techniques of avoiding masculinity by their parents. When a boy does not make excuses it is frequently because he does not need to—mom and dad do it for him. This is particularly the case when there have been consequences for the failure, whatever it is. Suppose the coach substitutes another player, or the boy is dropped from the team because he is on academic probation, or some other fallout occurs. Parents are often ferocious in "explaining" why this shouldn't happen. The son is in the background, taking notes. So when they, the parents, confront him about something, he does to them what he has already learned *from* them. What he has learned is the practice of refusing to take responsibility. He has learned how to reject masculinity. This can all be done in a loud voice, and with hairy chest, but it is still shirking a duty assigned by God.

At the same time, we should also distinguish excuse-making from giving an explanation which is called for. If mom asks her son why he was late for dinner, it is all right for him to tell her it was because he was hit by a car, and the emergency room wouldn't release him in time, and the phone at home was busy. But if mom asks why he was late, and he says that it was because the watch *she* gave him for his birthday is slow, and that it wasn't *his* fault, we have an example of the problem.

Boys must learn to say, regularly—to God, to others, and to themselves—that they were wrong when they were wrong, and that they were responsible when they were responsible. When they do this, they will discover that authority naturally flows to those who take responsibility. That same authority naturally flees from those who seek to shift the responsibility or the blame. When boys learn to do this, they are learning what it means to be a young man. When young men learn to do this, they are learning what it means to be a grown man.

Consequently, when a father asks his son why a particular chore was not accomplished, a good, normal response should be, "No excuse, sir." If this is said with the right demeanor, without insolence, without any spin on the word *sir*, then the son is learning what he needs to learn. The buck stops with him. The father should accept this and not badger him into excuse-making. So in its turn, the acceptance of responsibility should be *accepted*.

Another related problem is the practice of young men gravitating to one or two things they are naturally good at and staying there. Just as an excuse-maker will try to take credit only for the successes, so other young men will spend all their time in areas where excuse-making is not really necessary. The boy who dislikes academics gravitates to sports, and the boy who has trouble with music gives it a wide berth. The result is a very *narrow* competence, and the world outside that realm of competence is simply ignored.

This false masculinity—excuse-making, bluster, braggadocio—is in part the result of resisting and opposing true masculinity. Males will necessarily be dominant in any given culture, and the only question before that culture concerns whether or not that dominance will be constructive or destructive. If boys (and then later, men) are given a responsible, leadership role to play then the dominance will be constructive. But if this kind of responsible dominance is excluded by law, then boys will begin to dominate in a destructive way.

Keeping the Balance

Avoiding the extremes of effeminacy and macho-man reaction is very difficult. Our society is completely out of balance when it comes to understanding the roles of male and female. Trying to correct that imbalance without becoming unbalanced ourselves is a very hard task. But balance in marriage, balance in worship, balance in doctrine, and balance in individual practice are nevertheless required. At the same time, this balance is to be defined according to the Word, and not according to the moderate nervousness the world has about such complicated things.

> Therefore, if you died with Christ from the basic principles of the world, why, as though living in the world, do you subject yourselves to regulations— "Do not touch, do not taste, do not handle," which

all concern things which perish with the using—
according to the commandments and doctrines of
men? These things indeed have an appearance of
wisdom in self-imposed religion, false humility, and
neglect of the body, but are of no value against the
indulgence of the flesh. (Col. 2:20–23, NKJV)

Our tendency is to careen from one extreme to the
other. We see in this passage that ascetic reactions do not
check the indulgence of the flesh because they *are* an indulgence of the flesh. Pagans visit brothels to satisfy the flesh
while professing believers *do the same thing* through making
up rules not required by Scripture. Self-imposed religion,
what the older theologians used to call "will-worship," is an
abomination to God. Everything we do is to be to the glory
of God, defined by the revealed will of God. This sounds
very spiritual, but it is not that easy.

The first principle of balance is strict obedience. We must
never underestimate the importance of doing exactly what
God requires. God expressly forbids imitative innovations
in worship (Deut. 12:30–32); God struck down Nadab and
Abihu for offering strange incense (Lev. 10:1–2); Saul was
rejected as king because of his rebellion in taking Samuel's
place (1 Sam. 15:22–23); Uzza was struck down for touch-
ing the ark when the oxen stumbled (1 Chr. 13:9–10); King
Uzziah tried to burn incense before the Lord contrary to
the law and was struck with leprosy (2 Chr. 26:17–18); and
Hezekiah destroyed the bronze serpent (2 Kgs. 18:4). Zeal
in our religion is commanded (Tit. 2:14); in a very important
sense we are never to be moderate Christians. "So then,
because you are lukewarm, and neither cold nor hot, I will
spew you out of My mouth" (Rev. 3:16).

Another principle of balance, however, is just as important. We are obliged to obey strictly what God has said, not
what we *thought* He said, or what we assumed He said, or
what we thought he should have said. "He who sends a message by the hand of a fool cuts off his own feet and drinks
violence" (Prov. 26:6). Before we obey the Word, we must

know it to be the Word. As soon as we know it to be the Word, our responsibility for submission is immediate and complete.

Our goal is perfection, not perfectionism. The Word of God is absolute. But it is false to assume from this premise that the Bible provides a tidy list of do's and don'ts, all of which must accord with a respectable and middle class common sense. Although the law required priests to have a certain lineage which the usurping priests of Christ's day did not have, the Bible still treats Caiaphas as the genuine high priest (Jn. 11:51); Hezekiah requested that God receive certain defiled Israelites coming to the reinstituted Passover (2 Chr. 30:17–19); Namaan received permission to escort his master into the house of Rimmon, and there to help him bow (2 Kgs. 5:17–18); David unlawfully ate the showbread and was praised by Christ (Mt. 12:4); and Christians should have no trouble eating meat that was offered up to an idol (1 Cor. 8:4). Perfectionism has the appearance of wisdom, but it is a work of the flesh. We do not counter perfectionism with imperfectionism; we counter perfectionism with *obedience*.

These are the general principles; when we seek to balance masculinity in our sons with femininity in our daughters, we have to return constantly to what Scripture teaches. What does the Bible show us concerning masculinity? This is why we had to begin with the biblical categories—lord, husbandman, savior, sage, and glory. Taking all of Scripture together, these aspects of masculinity balance one another, and their corresponding complements in women provide still further balance.

CHAPTER THREE

A Call for Fathers

The problem which fathers face in the rearing of boys can be divided up into two categories. A wise father will recognize these various threats and will lead his wife as the two of them together seek to bring their son up in the nurture and admonition of the Lord.

Boys are threatened from two directions. Of course, like all sinners, they will be tempted from within. Rising to the challenges of manhood is very difficult, and the temptation to abdicate will arise whether or not anyone from the outside is encouraging it. We all tend to sin "downhill." Boys will frequently not assume the responsibilities assigned to them for the same reason we prefer riding a bicycle down the hill rather than up it.

At the same time, boys are confronted with a culture which is hostile to the very idea of masculinity and which is industriously doing whatever it can to exterminate it. Boys who, for whatever reason, resist the allurements of masculine laziness immediately find themselves at war with the culture at large. Boys must be protected from this onslaught while they are being trained to protect and defend themselves.

The Praise of Discipline

In order to counter both threats, a wise father *disciplines*. "For whom the lord loveth he correcteth; even as a father the son in whom he delighteth" (Prov. 3:12). This passage is encouragingly quoted in the book of Hebrews:

And ye have forgotten the exhortation which speaketh unto you as unto children, My son, despise not thou the chastening of the Lord, nor faint when thou art rebuked of him: For whom the Lord loveth he chasteneth, and scourgeth every son whom he receiveth. (Heb. 12:5–6)

The father here disciplines the son *in whom he delights*. Refusal to discipline amounts to hatred and is simply a slow, cruel way for a man to disown his son, clearly marking him out as illegitimate. True discipline is the foundation of respect—respect that will last a lifetime.

Related to this, a wise father rejoices in the fruit of his discipline. This is why many "disciplinarians" are not disciplinarians in the biblical sense at all. They discipline because they are annoyed or irritated; they are almost impossible to please and they go through life like a crate of crankcase oil. But a "wise son maketh a *glad* father: but a foolish son is the heaviness of his mother" (Prov. 10:1; cf. 15:20).

So strength in discipline by itself is not sufficient. A father must also be wise in how he uses his strength. Many strong, aggressive fathers are very foolish in how they use that strength with their boys. Strong men are frequently competitive men, and competitive men are often competitive with their sons. And this is why many "strong" fathers have weak sons—the son was never allowed to attempt anything. Or, when he attempted something, it was never good enough, and the "disciplinary" response was always disproportionate and unjust. Discipline of this sort comes from fathers who are control freaks, having to do everything themselves, or having it turn out as though they had.

A disciplining father delights in his son. A neglectful or abdicating father despises his son. An overbearing father despises his son as well, and it does him no good to cling to those verses which talk about discipline. Discipline without wisdom is destructive.

This means that a wise father is one who is capable of praising his son and showing joy in his accomplishments.

"The father of the righteous shall greatly rejoice: and he that begetteth a wise child shall have joy of him. Thy father and thy mother shall be glad, and she that bare thee shall rejoice" (Prov. 23:24–25; cf. 29:3).

A wise father teaches—a lot. In the context of church, we know that the Word must also accompany the sacrament. In a similar way, the word must always accompany the discipline. Fathers must teach their sons—the point of discipline is not to retaliate against a boy. The justice involved in familial discipline is not retributive—there is no question of "getting back." The point of discipline is to gain an audience, and there is no sense in gaining an audience if you then do not say anything. Fathers are to teach, and they are to teach receptive sons. The way the receptivity is gained is through discipline, but discipline is not an end in itself. A godly home should contain discipline, not retribution.

Disciplining Toward Dominion

Godly discipline in general has to have a focus. Fathers are especially called to discipline their sons to be *lords,* as discussed earlier. In particular, sons must learn to fulfill the cultural mandate in a masculine manner.

Genesis is the book of beginnings, too often neglected by Christians. Here we see the beginning of the world, obviously, but also the beginning of marriage, rest, music, and for our purposes here—work. The word *vocation* comes from the Latin *voco,* meaning "I call." Your son's vocation is therefore his *calling* under God. He is to be prepared for that vocation, and the preparation will not go well when parents do not understand the point of it.

Then God blessed them, and God said to them, "Be fruitful and multiply; fill the earth and subdue it; have dominion over the fish of the sea, over the birds of the air, and over every living thing that moves on the earth." (Gen. 1:28)

So God blessed Noah and his sons, and said to them:
"Be fruitful and multiply, and fill the earth. And the
fear of you and the dread of you shall be on every
beast of the earth, on every bird of the air, on all
that move on the earth, and on all the fish of the sea.
They are given into your hand. Every moving thing
that lives shall be food for you. I have given you all
things, even as the green herbs." (Gen. 9:1–3)

These commands from God have traditionally been
called the cultural mandate. Before the Fall, God expressly
gave dominion to mankind over all creation. This is seen
in the passage from the first chapter of Genesis. But God
reiterates this charge to Noah—Noah lived after the Fall,
and this mandate is given immediately after a stupendous
judgment on sin. Consequently, the presence of sin obviously does not lift or remove the cultural mandate.

Moreover, the language of the mandate assumes that
generations downstream will continue to operate in terms
of this mandate. Consider the words of Psalm 8. Contrary
to the modern "green" assumptions, man is not an intruder
on this planet. We are stewards; care of this world is en-
trusted to us. We belong here.

Sin affected our ability to fulfill the cultural mandate;
it did not alter our obligation to fulfill it. And a central part
of the reason Christ came was to restore mankind and the
vocation of mankind. The author of the book of Hebrews
takes this passage from Psalm 8 and applies it to mankind in
Christ. Consider his application of the psalm. The mandate
remains in force for impotent man—but that impotence is
removed in Christ.

For He has not put the world to come, of which we
speak, in subjection to angels. . . . You have made him
a little lower than the angels; You have crowned him
with glory and honor, and set him over the works
of Your hands. You have put all things in subjection
under his feet. For in that He put all in subjection
under him, He left nothing that is not put under

him. But now we do not yet see all things put under him. (Heb. 2:5–8)

Now a son is part of this mandate—God's call to him includes his vocation. What he does is not just a detached "job" (Eph. 2:8–10). We must confess the sin of parceling up the world, along with the desire to have some of the parcels (like our jobs) to be "Christless." When a son is trained rightly, he understands that Christ is Lord and has been given a name above every name. He is the Lord of *all*—and we cannot think He is somehow not Lord of our occupations. If we do, it is time to think again (Phil. 2:9–11; 1 Pet. 3:22; Heb. 12:2; Eph. 1:19–21).

We must recognize that this mandate is to a masculine vocation in the world. A son's wife, of course, is essential to this process—he cannot do without her help (Gen. 2:18). Being a good husband is the most important aspect of fulfilling the cultural mandate, though other aspects will show up through this book. As a young man prepares for marriage, he needs to be confident that he has the necessary strength. Women are created by God to be led by a strong man, but marriage is disastrous when a man is not strong enough, or his strength is not biblically informed.

Part of the curse in Genesis is seen in how the woman desires to have mastery over her husband. When God tells Eve that her desire will be for her husband (Gen. 3:16), this was not referring to romantic getaways. The phrase is virtually identical to the one found in the next chapter, when God warns Cain that sin wants to have mastery over him (Gen. 4:7). On one level, women want to rule their husbands (as a result of the fall), but on another level entirely (because of the created order), they have a deep desire to be protected and led by a man who is strong enough. A young man is not ready for marriage unless he knows this, and knows that he has sufficient horsepower to pull that load.

So an essential part of the preparation for a young man as he considers the cultural mandate is his training for marriage. Future men are future husbands. The foundation of respect here is a foundation of love. When we look at what God requires of men and women in marriage, we are looking at what fathers and mothers should be preparing their sons and daughters to do when they are grown. A boy should not grow up—*however* he manages that—and then when he gets engaged start worrying about how to be a good husband. Knowledge of what a godly husband is should surround him from the time he is a small boy.

The center of godly demeanor in marriage is love as the central duty of husbands and respect as the central duty of wives. The husband is to love his wife as Christ loved the church. A wife should respect and honor her husband as the church does to Christ. This exemplifies the gospel in an incarnational way. A good husband knows how to give love, and he knows how to receive respect. Just as he ought to love his wife, so he *needs* to love his wife. Just as he ought to receive respect from his wife, so he *needs* to receive respect from her. And what he knows how to do, boys need to learn how to do.

Fathers are therefore to discipline their sons on the path to manhood. They are to delight in their boys as they pass by certain milestones on the way to manhood, and they are to teach them as they walk along the way together. This is not easy.

This is a great need in the Christian church today—we have a dearth of genuine fathers. We have males who have begotten more males, but we do not have many true *fathers*. Many men who should now be training their boys to be men are not yet men themselves. The gauntlet which their boys need to run is a gauntlet which they themselves failed to run. The battle their sons face is a battle which they once faced, and lost. Because of this, many of the lessons about masculinity contained in Scripture must first be internalized by the fathers. Such men must learn to be men themselves before they can teach their boys to be men.

This is a moral obligation, and, as such, failure to meet it calls for repentance, not merely an intellectual shuffling of categories. Learning which follows repentance is just what we need, but learning as a substitute for repentance is just another way of wimping out. Fathers who discipline must themselves be under discipline.

But the full measure of training boys is not left to fathers alone; it is the effort of the whole covenant household, the subject of the next chapter.

CHAPTER FOUR

A Covenant Home

When a boy grows up in a believing household, this does not mean that no snares threaten him. Though many children are born into covenant homes, *no one* is born into a place of automatic spiritual safety. A covenant home is the ideal place, if the parents are obedient, for a son to learn to avoid making the wrong assumptions.

"My son, if thine heart be wise, my heart shall rejoice, even mine. Yea, my reins shall rejoice, when thy lips speak right things" (Prov. 23:15–16). Of course the same lessons are available to daughters. "Many daughters have done virtuously, but thou excellest them all. Favour is deceitful, and beauty is vain: but a woman that feareth the LORD, she shall be praised" (Prov. 31:29–30).

The obligation to fear and serve God in truth does not begin at a certain age. As long as we have breath, we must praise the Lord. As long as we live among the covenant people of God, we share their covenantal obligations. Many young boys in the faith have a false assumption about all this; they think that walking with God *someday* is inevitable, but they think they can postpone that day of reckoning—they don't believe they have to "grow up" yet. This assumption is reinforced throughout the Bible belt, where a culture of rededication has taken root. Young men are expected to sow their wild oats, and then, in due time, to come back to the fold, rededicating their lives.

But obedience (whether someone is mature or not) is never optional. And when our sons learn wisdom and live accordingly, they bring joy and praise. We can't grasp this, though, unless we're grounded in covenantal thinking.

Foundation for Respect

Rearing boys is a covenantal task. As parents undertake it, they should understand how the concept of covenant defines and shapes this task. So we will begin by defining the idea of covenant biblically, and then showing how it applies to however many boys are gathered around the dining room table.

Our Bibles can be divided into two sections—the Old Testament or Covenant and the New Testament or New Covenant. A good indicator of the condition of the modern evangelical church can be seen in the fact that many believers do not understand what this refers to. What does this word *covenant* mean?

A covenant is simply a solemn bond, sovereignly administered, with attendant blessings and curses. With this definition, we must still consider the outworking of God's covenants with men throughout history. We are faced with two basic options. Either God has made one basic covenant with men throughout history, or He has made more than one—possibly many. As we shall see, Scripture teaches that God has made one basic covenant with fallen men throughout history, which we may call the covenant of grace. In the New Testament, we see the proper scriptural final name for this covenant is the New Covenant.

Before the Fall, God had made a covenant with mankind in Adam, which we all violated through our sin. Genesis tells us that Adam sinned against God, but Hosea tells us that Adam sinned against God covenantally. "But like men they transgressed the covenant; there they dealt treacherously with Me" (Hos. 6:7). The word translated *men* here is the Hebrew word for *Adam*.

In redemptive history, God makes covenants throughout the Old Testament. But they are not a series of disconnected covenants, as though God kept changing His mind

about how to deal with men. His covenants unfold succes-
sively, and they cannot be understood apart from one another. He did this first with Adam and Eve—"And I will
put enmity between you and the woman, and between your
seed and her Seed; He shall bruise your head, and you shall
bruise His heel" (Gen. 3:15). We know from the New Testament that this is a messianic promise (e.g., Rom. 16:20),
which means it must be understood covenantally. He speaks
again to Noah: "But I will establish My covenant with you;
and you shall go into the ark—you, your sons, your wife,
and your sons' wives with you" (Gen. 6:18). Peter clearly
tells us that this was a type, and that Christian baptism
is the antitype (1 Pet. 3:18–22). This also was part of the
redemptive covenant.

God also makes a covenant with Abraham—"And I
will make My covenant between Me and you, and will multiply you exceedingly" (Gen. 17:2). As the New Testament
tells us in multiple places, Abraham is the father of all who
believe (Rom. 4:11). Moreover, the Bible tells us that "if
you are Christ's, then you are Abraham's seed, and heirs
according to the promise" (Gen. 3:29). The implications
of this are profound. We see that God remembered His
covenant with Abraham in the covenant He made through
Moses—"So God heard their groaning, and God remembered His covenant with Abraham, with Isaac, and with
Jacob. And God looked upon the children of Israel, and
God acknowledged them" (Exod. 2:24–25). Understanding the ramifications of this passage is crucial to a proper
grasp of the teaching of the New Testament. The covenant
with Moses was *not* separated from the others; neither was
it a detour.

God also gave a wonderful covenantal promise to David—
"When your days are fulfilled and you rest with your fathers,
I will set up your seed after you, who will come from your
body, and I will establish his kingdom" (2 Sam. 7:12–16).
Who is the Christ? He is the Son of David.

All these covenants were a covenantal prelude to the coming of the Christ. Believers should not think of separated pacts or contracts throughout history. The believer must think of a growing child, a fruitful tree, a bud unfolding into a flower. We must understand *the continuity of the covenants over generations*. That continuity is found in a Person and reflects the solitary redemptive purpose of God from the beginning of history to the end of it, always expressed in covenant. The Lord Jesus Christ is the Lord of the New Covenant now (Heb. 8:6), He has always been the Lord of the New Covenant (1 Cor. 10:1–13), and He ministers the benefits of it throughout all history (Heb. 9:15).

This serves as the backdrop for some meddling. In our culture, in our time, as we consider the relationship of youth to age, we have both perennial problems (obviously) and problems that are unique to our time. The covenant home is the place where the truth about such things is to be figured out.

Covenant Temptations

The first great task confronting parents today is to bring their children up within the covenant, and in such a way as their children feel a lifelong loyalty to that covenant. This task addresses the question of whether our children will be Christians after us, and whether they will bring up their children in the Christian faith. But once this question is settled, numerous temptations remain. Of course Christian parents should remember the possibility of failure. But wise parents will remember that temptations also come with success.

When considering our "covenant temptations," we have to divide the subject into two categories. The first concerns the mistakes about the very nature of covenant thinking as it applies to child rearing. The second category involves more mundane temptations from within the covenant. The former is a theological problem, and the latter is simply what might be called an ordinary sin problem.

The theological mistake which is commonly made about the nature of the covenant is that of assuming that our boys are aliens to the obligations of the covenant when they are born into our homes, and that they incur no covenantal obligations until they make an individual choice to "sign up." But the Bible teaches that the children of at least one believing parent are to be considered *saints* (1 Cor. 7:14). A son does not have to join the covenant; the sovereign God has already joined him to the covenant people of God by placing him in a believing home. Of course, such a boy must have what we might call evangelical faith in order to maintain his covenantal membership. But he does not have to prove himself in order to join the covenant. When parents accept and believe this, they bring up their sons to believe, rather than teaching them to doubt.

And this brings us to sinful assumptions which are commonly made from within the covenant.

Ignorance and Laziness: In our age, wisdom is simply assumed to reside with youth. According to this current assumption, wisdom is not acquired through decades of faithful obedience but was issued (somehow) with the kid's driver's license. This is a lie (Prov. 22:15). A young man's mother starts to tell him something, so he rolls his eyes and says, "I know, I *know*" (Prov. 18:13). Not only is this a lie, it has been a very successful one.

Ignorance also shows itself in laziness. Being indoctrinated in the jargon of a particular branch of the faith is easy. Many sons of the readers of this book have no doubt learned to mouth all sorts of covenant words, which is not the same thing as being able to think.

Some children unthinkingly accept everything they are taught. Such a child encounters an atheist for the first time, both of them being around eleven years old, and so he says something like, "I suppose you're an evolutionist too. Duh."

Kids like this have not really been taught and discipled, but only successfully propagandized. One of the key marks of such victims of propaganda is their *facile readiness* to apply the tenets of the faith to others. Those who dispute its doctrines are considered to be simply stupid, those who reject its ethical teachings are the equivalent of cannibalistic axe-murderers, and so on. Such ignorance stems from laziness.

Presumption and Boasting: Throughout the Bible, we are warned about the sins of covenantal presumption. A young man is not a permanent branch on the olive tree just because his parents are (Rom. 11:13–24). He should take particular care here if he is growing up in a paedobaptist home. Unexamined assumptions can be deadly. Related to this is the problem of covenant doubts. God requires young people to serve Him honestly and from the heart. He does not require them to wait until later (Eph. 6:1–3). A young man should take particular care here if he is growing up in a baptistic home. Parents are instructed to bring their children to the faith, not to the doubts.

Presumption takes other forms as well. Boys brought up in the truth are particularly prone to know-it-all chatter. Truth is rigid and unyielding and is almost as good as a baseball bat for hitting people with. I have seen this happen so frequently with Christian young men that I have decided to name the phenomenon—they should be called "thunder puppies." Jesus once rebuked His disciples because they wanted to declare celestial war, calling down fire from heaven, but yet, they did not know what spirit they were of. In the same way today, many young men preach beyond their wisdom and pronounce dogmatically beyond their years.

Many young Christian men will go on and on about what they will require their (hypothetical) wives to do in this or that situation, and how *they* will homeschool, and what they will demand of anyone who dares interfere with their sacrosanct household. And compare this to how often they spend time talking about what they will require of *themselves.* In short, "thunder puppies" are too ready to boast about nonexistent accomplishments and to bring others down in the process.

But to begin with others is not the biblical order. "Brethren, if a man be overtaken in a fault, ye which are spiritual, restore such an one in the spirit of meekness; considering thyself, lest thou also be tempted" (Gal. 6:1). When another person must be corrected, it is only to be undertaken by those who are spiritual, and they are to make sure of a meek and gentle spirit, watching over their own heart, lest they fall into sin as well. This is a hard task when someone has grown up perpetually disgusted with secular humanists who don't believe the Bible. The disgust often serves as a camo-cover which hides the fact that the young man in question doesn't believe the Bible either—at least not those portions which apply to him.

Of course the world is a sinful place, and we want our young men taught and equipped to enable them to rise up to battle when the situation calls for it. As we have seen, the Bible teaches us that the glory of young men is their strength. But a careful contrast reveals the beauty of the old man, which is the wisdom of a gray head (Prov. 20:29). That wisdom sees that boasting is never profitable, unless it is in the Lord.

Handled wrongly, a Christian upbringing for a young man can provide many opportunities to show how those darn "other people" do not do what the Bible says. "Boast not thyself of tomorrow; for thou knowest not what a day may bring forth. Let another man praise thee, and not thine own mouth; a stranger, and not thine own lips" (Prov. 27:1–2).

A covenant home should not only guard against these problems, it should also constructively prepare sons for war. Though a young man has a unique station in life, he is nonetheless called to discipleship together with the rest of us. As he develops a Christian life, he should do so by receiving instruction from his parents, elders, and his other betters, along with anyone else who has something biblical to teach. A young man should *listen to it* (Prov. 1:3).

As he does so, he needs to believe the promises; growing in discipleship means learning to walk by faith and not by works. This means he is to be motivated through believing God's gracious promises (Eph. 6:2).

In other words, he must set his mind for the battle. He was born to warfare in a world which is in the process of being subdued to the Word of God. He imitates the Lord Jesus Christ. A young man must learn his weapons, learn his armor, and learn his tactics. Central to that is the topic of the next chapter.

CHAPTER FIVE

Doctrinal Meat

As they grow up, young men are to be prepared for the spiritual warfare that awaits them. They have to learn their responsibilities as part of the kingdom. "Both young men and maidens; old men and children. Let them praise the name of the Lord, for His name alone is exalted; His glory is above the earth and heaven" (Ps. 148:12–13).

The first thing to note is that the kingdom of God is not divided. The members of various subgroups are certainly distinguished from each other, and they are treated differently with regard to their social relations. But the basic responsibility of all—men and women, young men and young women, boys and girls, remains the same—to worship the Lord. Our tendency is to say things like, "Oh, well, at *his* age you can't really expect this." But this is radically unbiblical. Everything that breathes has an obligation to praise the Lord; no exemptions have been granted for teenage boys. The Bible knows nothing of a normal alienation between generations.

The blessings which flow from such faithful worship are not limited to those who are older. "The Lord their God will save them in that day, as the flock of His people. For they shall be like the jewels of a crown, lifted like a banner over His land—for how great is its goodness and how great its beauty! *Grain shall make the young men thrive*, and new wine the young women" (Zech. 9:16–17). When God is blessing a people, *all* are included in His bounty.

The same thing is true when the judgment of God comes upon a people. God does *not* just judge or chastise those who are eighteen and older. We are organically connected; when the hand of the Lord is upon us, we are all affected. Jeremiah says this about a time of reckoning. "Therefore I am full of the fury of the Lord. I am weary of holding it in. 'I will pour it out on the children outside, *and on the assembly of young men together*; for even the husband shall be taken with the wife, the aged with him who is full of days'" (Jer. 6:11). When a society stands, the whole society stands. When it falls, everyone in it falls with it.

Young Men Singled Out

Not only is this the case, but each particular subset of a culture brings its own contributions and liabilities. Men bring one thing, women another, young women still another, and so forth. In this regard, the "glory of young men is their strength, and the splendor of old men is their gray head" (Prov. 20:29). An old man is distinguished in wisdom. This is his splendor. Young men are not so distinguished, but God has compensated them with the glory of strength. As they are called to their duties, they are not to lean on their own understanding. They are not to be bullheaded, and they must use the strength God gave them to throw themselves into obedience.

These social distinctions among us mean that different groups are regularly singled out in Scripture with admonition or teaching which suits a particular need. God commands to our weaknesses. "Likewise exhort the young men *to be sober-minded*, in all things showing yourself to be a pattern of good works; in doctrine showing integrity, reverence, incorruptibility, sound speech that cannot be condemned, that one who is an opponent may be ashamed, having nothing evil to say of you" (Tit. 2:6–8). Titus here is told to exhort the young men to be sober-minded (the word is *sophroneo*, and indicates a certain modesty of mind). Titus is then told to set an example for these young men.

Those things which are to be included in his example for the young men are noteworthy.

Doctrinal Integrity: The teaching of the church must have integrity. A teacher must not be guilty of trifling with the text, or of special pleading which keeps certain doctrines at bay. A young man watching this will learn to hold the Scriptures in the same contempt that the teacher apparently does. This, incidentally is a lesson being taught (and learned) in churches all over our nation. Our doctrine is without integrity, and our boys grow up without having seen a pattern of any kind of doctrinal integrity.

Reverence: A man should conduct himself in all things with dignity, and young men should learn to conduct themselves with dignity. This does not mean young men should be dour, but it does exclude the general fruitiness that we have come to cultivate among the young. Young men should long for the dignity of maturity. They must not buy into the current pattern of perpetuating youthful immaturity in dress, manners, and so forth.

Incorruptibility: Titus was told to abhor every form of dishonesty, which in turn sets a necessary pattern for the young men. A young man should learn to be incorruptible. He must be *scrupulous* in all his dealings, absolutely honest in his schoolwork, above board with money, one who knows how to sweat honestly, and one who hates the very idea of lying to cover up sexual corruptions.

Sound Speech: Titus was told to model sound speech—which probably meant that he never said things like, "Like, dude, like, an awesome thing, dude, is the fact that, man, I like, totally don't know what to say."

Focus on Doctrinal Integrity

Returning to the issue of doctrinal integrity, young men first need to have a solid grasp of the parts of a Christian worldview, and especially two issues in particular—the sovereignty of God and an optimistic view of the future.

To start, what is a Christian worldview? The use of popular words is always dangerous. As words enter into common currency, they can soon cease to be helpful as they rapidly become "buzzwords"—words that evoke a certain immediate response, but which still remain nebulous and undefined. *Worldview* is in danger of becoming just such a word; it is certainly used a lot, but do we really have a clear idea of what we mean by it? Perhaps a brief overview will whet the appetite for more.

Paul says, "For though we walk in the flesh, we do not war according to the flesh. For the weapons of our warfare are not carnal but mighty in God for pulling down strongholds, casting down arguments and every high thing that exalts itself against the knowledge of God, bringing every thought into captivity to the obedience of Christ, and being ready to punish all disobedience when your obedience is fulfilled" (2 Cor. 10:3–6). A Christian worldview is therefore a framework of assumptions about reality, all of which are in submission to Christ. A Christian worldview is *not* defined as a worldview held by someone who is a Christian. Christians can do "non-Christian" actions, and in the same way, Christians can certainly think "non-Christian" thoughts. Consequently, we have to learn how to distinguish Christian from non-Christian thought, and the criterion for distinction cannot be that the former is what occurs within Christian heads.

The basic framework of the Christian worldview includes, first and foremost, the gospel. This consists of two basic parts—knowing the condition of man and knowing the provision of God in Christ. Man is dead, not sick, in his sins (Eph. 2:1–2). The God/man in Christ has died on the cross for His people (Eph. 5:25) and was raised to life for their justification (Rom. 4:25) in accordance with the Scripture (1 Cor. 15:1–4). In short, the gospel is about *knowing God in covenant*. The gospel brings individuals into a covenant relationship with God.

In understanding God in covenant, a Christian worldview will show how the reality of the Trinity, Incarnation,

Creator/creature distinction, atonement, Church, etc., shape the world ways that make Christianity unique. In delving deeper into these truths, a young man should begin to recognize how they produce different answers to questions in history, literature, philosophy, the sciences, and every day-to-day question. Books discussing the nature of the Christian worldview are quite plentiful these days. But two aspects of Christian theology stand out for particular attention here because of their connection to *masculinity*: the sovereignty of God and an optimistic future.

Sovereignty: The Bible teaches that God controls everything, and nothing will build a young man's spine more thoroughly than this doctrine, along with the ramifications of it. God views all that we do. "For the ways of man are before the eyes of the LORD, and He ponders all his paths" (Prov. 5:21). God watches everything that men do. "The eyes of the LORD are in every place, keeping watch on the evil and the good" (Prov. 15:3). We see here that God *watches* the commission of wickedness. If we are competent to judge God for His perfect control of evil, then why do we stop there? Why not judge Him for His refusal to intervene? The text here says that He watches the commission of evil. Wouldn't *we* be blameworthy if we did that?

We also see the liberty of God in knowing the heart of man. "Hell and Destruction are before the LORD; so how much more the hearts of the sons of men" (Prov. 15:11). "The thoughts of the wicked are an abomination to the LORD, but the words of the pure are pleasant" (Prov. 15:26). "Every way of a man is right in his own eyes, but the LORD weighs the hearts" (Prov. 21:2). God is not a mere spectator of the outside of a man. He sees all the way in. As sin is conceived in the mind, this brings us back to the point made in the previous section.

The Bible teaches that God has complete sovereignty over inanimate things. "The lot is cast into the lap, but its every decision is from the LORD" (Prov. 16:33). We must note that Solomon does not tell us what each decision means— just that it is from the Lord. We must distinguish here between the decretive will of God (heads or tails), and the moral will of God—what He tells us to do in His Word.

God's sovereignty over all things does not disappear when evil is involved. "The LORD has made all for Himself, yes, even the wicked for the day of doom. Everyone proud in heart is an abomination to the LORD; though they join forces, none will go unpunished" (Prov. 16:4–5). We see how the Word does not oppose God's exhaustive sovereignty and man's responsibility to one another. We must take care that our boys not fall either into the errors of hyper-Calvinism or Arminianism.

God also has full liberty in His control of free actions. "The preparations of the heart belong to man, but the answer of the tongue is from the LORD" (Prov. 16:1). God controls what we say. "A man's heart plans his way, but the LORD directs his steps" (Prov. 16:9). God controls where we step—this includes the gas pedal, and this is why we pray for traveling mercies. It does not depend upon a "yielded heart." When a man's ways please the LORD, He makes even his enemies to be at peace with him" (Prov. 16:7).

God controls the devising of a man's heart. "The king's heart is in the hand of the LORD, like the rivers of water; He turns it wherever He wishes" (Prov. 21:1). God's control is not limited to externals. He turns the heart of the king any direction, and there is no hint of any diminution of the king's responsibility.

In short, these passages mean that *God controls everything.* "There is no wisdom or understanding or counsel against the LORD" (Prov. 21:30). God cannot be outsmarted; under no circumstances can His decretive will be thwarted—and remember the distinction made above concerning His will. "There are many plans in a man's heart, nevertheless the LORD's counsel—that will stand" (Prov. 19:21; cf. 21:31; 22:2; 26:10; 29:13).

How God can do this is beyond us. "A man's steps are of the LORD; how then can a man understand his own way?" (Prov. 20:24). Our boys need to learn humility, and they also need to learn boldness and courage. The only way to accomplish this in balance is through a grasp of who God is. Because we have ceased teaching that God is our *Father*, with the attributes of a divine *father*, we have lost an understanding of imitative masculinity. Because of this, our boys veer into one of two ditches. Either they embrace humility without boldness, which in boys is effeminate, or they embrace boldness without humility, which is destructive. *Optimism:* Jesus told us that the meek will inherit the earth. This meekness is Godward and should not be confused with a man-ward weakness or effeminacy. "Blessed are the meek." These are familiar words. As familiar words, they have much in common with other well-traveled passages. One common feature is the fact that the promise is not well-understood. The word to us is very clear—"Blessed are the meek, for they shall inherit the earth." A blessing is pronounced upon a certain kind of individual. Again, this is not speaking of someone who is weak, shy, or naturally retiring. The virtue or grace spoken of is a spiritual meekness, humility, and lowliness. Those with this demeanor are blessed because they will inherit the earth.

As Christians, we are to understand meekness first by imitation. Our Lord himself is our example (Mt. 11:29). He is gentle. But such meekness or gentleness is not inconsistent with strength. We must imitate the Lord in all things. We see a lesser example in Moses. He was a strong and decisive leader, and yet the Word says that he was very humble (Num. 12:3). By imitating scriptural examples, we will not fall into the error of trying to isolate one grace from all the others and living it out to an extreme. When we fall into this error, we mistakenly urge weakness upon our boys in the name of spirituality. Not surprisingly, they resist this. But meekness, biblically understood, equips them for the mission in the world which God has assigned to them. The meek will inherit the *earth*, which means that the Christian faith is a religion of world conquest.

Toward God, meekness means we must have a teachable spirit. It cannot be said too strongly that this teachable spirit is teachable before God. This meekness toward God can look like arrogance to those who do not care about the will of God. Meekness which is Godward is strength on earth. In displaying this kind of meekness, we must be ready to submit to the providential will of God as revealed in events, and we must be ready to submit to the revealed will of God as displayed in His Word. The former is seen in the example of Job (Job 1:20–22), and the latter is seen in the words of Christ in the previous chapter (Job 4:4). Meekness is not weakness before man. It is submission to God, which equips a young man to stand tall and upright before lawless thrones, as three young men once did in Babylon.

Meekness toward others means, among other things, that we must refuse to be provoked by others. "Those who seek my hurt speak of destruction — but I, like a deaf man, do not hear" (Ps. 38:12-13; cf. Prov. 19:11). We must forgive others. We must not seek to receive forgiveness without extending it. But Christ has closed that door to His followers (Mt. 6:12). We must forgive really (all the way down), fully (across the board), and often (as often as we are wronged). Why? This is how God forgives us. And last, we must love others. "Let this mind be in you" (Phil. 2:5).

Having defined meekness, we need to return to the astounding promise. Jesus says that the meek will inherit the earth. We must not turn this upside down in our minds. Suppose someone tried to do this with the first part of this Beatitude. Suppose they said, "Blessed are the proud, for they will inherit the earth." Intolerable, we say. But these words are commonly distorted, and in just the same way. We think that the blessing is upon those who are meek, for "they will inherit heaven when they die." But this is not what Christ said. He said that the meek will inherit the earth.

The Old Testament prophesies that the coming days of the Christian era will be glorious indeed. Just one example:

"All the ends of the world shall remember and turn to the Lord, and all the families of the nations shall worship before You. For the kingdom is the Lord's, and He rules over the nations" (Ps. 22:27–28). Christ commands His followers to disciple the nations (Mt. 28:19). What do you suppose He meant by that? Perhaps He meant that we were supposed to disciple the nations.

The apostle Paul treats this as a commonly understood doctrine and appeals to it in order to teach Christians to avoid lawsuits before unbelievers. He says, "Do you not know that the saints will judge the world?" Modern Christians say, "Um, no, we didn't know that. Is that in the Bible?" The writer of Hebrews encourages the saints with visions of conquest (Heb. 12:25–29). But keeping our hearts and minds set on this passage from the Beatitudes, we must remember that these weapons are not carnal, they are not earthly, and they are not political. Blessed are the *meek*, for they shall inherit the earth.

If they are taught, boys will respond to a clear statement of the mission before the church. *Boys are built for battle*, and they must be trained up to it. But if we continue to teach the hopelessness of all our earthly endeavors, we must not be surprised when those among us who are built, created, for earthly endeavors, take their strength elsewhere. "Why do boys not like to come to church?" we wonder. The answer is that we chase them out with our insipid and impotent doctrine.

Put simply, our boys cannot learn how to become Christian men, men with doctrinal backbone, without a return to the doctrines of the Reformation, doctrines which are taught, and taught plainly, in the Scriptures.

CHAPTER SIX

Secret Sin, Tolerated Sin

Godly parents do not have the luxury of wanting to "not know" about sin their sons may have drifted into. If a son is starting to run with bad companions, or if he is starting to find porn on the net, or if he falling into a pattern of lies, they have to *want* to know about it. And one of their regular prayers should be that God would give them any information they need to know in order to be good parents.

And like Moses, they should warn their children about God's moral government of the world. Boys should grow up knowing that sin cannot ever be truly covered up.

> But if you do not do so, then take note, you have sinned against the LORD; and *be sure your sin will find you out.* (Num. 32:23)

If young men begin to nurture secret sin in their lives, then they have forgotten (or have not been taught) certain basic truths from God's Word. The Bible teaches us about the omniscience, the omnipotence, and the holiness of God. "And there is no creature hidden from His sight, but all things are naked and open to the eyes of Him to whom we must give account" (Heb. 4:13). The principle here is that secret sin is built upon a false theology of God. This false theology is not what we would call an honest mistake either; this kind of sin is driven by a willfulness which does not want the "invasive" God of orthodoxy.

We should also teach our boys to remember the sober warning of Christ:

Beware of the leaven of the Pharisees, which is hypocrisy. For there is nothing covered that will not be revealed, nor hidden that will not be known. Therefore whatever you have spoken in the dark will be heard in the light, and what you have spoken in the ear in inner rooms will be proclaimed on the housetops. (Lk. 12:1–3)

The principle here is that secret sin is only *temporarily* secret sin. God is not mocked, and a man reaps what he sows. Frequently that reaping is a very public matter. A late night party with the guys, that no one needs to know about, winds up in court with a young man facing a DUI charge. A young man gets a girl pregnant; they are both expelled from the Christian school they attend. The sin is no longer a secret matter. There was a time when earthly knowledge of the sin was confined to the back seat of the car. But God has promised to publicize things we would rather keep secret.

Another problem is that tolerating a little secret sin is like being a little bit pregnant.

So David sent and inquired about the woman. And someone said, "Is this not Bathsheba, the daughter of Eliam, the wife of Uriah the Hittite?" Then David sent messengers, and took her; and she came to him, and he lay with her, for she was cleansed from her impurity; and she returned to her house. . . . In the morning it happened that David wrote a letter to Joab and sent it by the hand of Uriah. And he wrote in the letter, saying, "Set Uriah in the forefront of the hottest battle, and retreat from him, that he may be struck down and die." (2 Sam. 11:3–4, 14–15)

Sin breeds sin, and hidden sin breeds more hidden sin. But as sin accumulates, it becomes impossible for the sinner to "manage." So the principle is that secret sin grows. When it grows, it assumes a form that is not nearly as pleasant as the initial sin was.

In other words, the sinner often wants to commit a certain number of initial sins, and has no desire to commit others. David was not driven by any particular animus toward Uriah. *Circumstances* ran over Uriah—but David was still at the wheel. A young man wants to make out with a girl—he didn't want to be a father when he was sixteen. A young man wanted to have fun with the guys joyriding—he didn't want to kill the little girl in the crosswalk. Sin consistently grows into something uglier than the initially attractive sin. Boys also need to learn the effect of hidden sin on others.

But the children of Israel committed a trespass regarding the accursed things, for Achan the son of Carmi, the son of Zabdi, the son of Zerah, of the tribe of Judah, took of the accursed things; so the anger of the LORD burned against the children of Israel. (Josh. 7:1)

Individuals who hide their sin are often guilty of another sin as well—the sin of individualism. That is, they believe that what they do affects only them. This is false. When a young man sins, his family now contains that sin. When he sins, his church sins. When he hides his sin, the corporate covenantal entities to which he is attached are also "hiding" sin. This is why the Lord required, in His law, a sacrifice for unsolved murders. The principle is that secret sin is never "contained" or "isolated" to one individual.

But God is merciful, and He will forgive young men who have been discovered in the grip of secret sin. Three solutions present themselves; the first two are false and one is true. The first false solution is to continue to hide the sin, on one's own terms, and in one's own way. But Moses' words should follow all who seek this way out—"be sure your sin will find you out." The second seeks to combine biblical truths with pragmatic solutions. "I confessed it to *God*. What else has to be done?" Sometimes there is nothing else but to receive forgiveness. But in other situations, much remains to be done—like restitution, confession to injured parties, and so forth.

The third way, the only way, is to want God's mercy so much that you are willing do exactly what He says when you apply to Him for it. And that means full and honest confession. This does not mean that everything is automatically fixed through an act of "mental obedience" alone. But it does begin there.

Accompanying this confession of sin is the young man's decision to apply himself to the means of grace—preparing himself for worship, listening attentively to the sermons, and coming gratefully and expectantly to the Lord's table. During the week, it means receiving instruction from parents, praying daily, reading the Bible on a consistent basis, and so forth.

Open Sin

But not all sin is hidden away. In many homes there is another category, that of open, tolerated sin. This is usually tolerated verbal sin—words spoken around the house. There are many aspects to this because we sin more with our mouths than any other way. "Whoever guards his mouth and tongue keeps his soul from troubles" (Prov. 21:23). Strife, quarrels, broken friendships, wounded friends, all come from sins of the tongue. Whenever Christians begin to act in a way that does not honor the Lord, almost always we may assume that someone is dispensing some bad whiskey.

Boys must be taught a right standard. In all conversation, we must remember the antithesis between true and false, right and wrong. Nothing is true because "someone said it," and nothing is false because "a man said it." Proverbs distinguishes, sharply, between the words of the wise and the words of the fool. "The tongue of the wise uses knowledge rightly, but the mouth of fools pours forth foolishness" (Prov. 15:2).

Remember that a fool does not identify himself as such. "The way of a fool is right in his own eyes" (Prov. 12:15).

We must always hold all words up against the light of Scripture. As we do so, we will find ourselves dealing with the situation as it is and not as it might be at some point in the future, in someone's imagination.

"Verbal scribbling" is another common problem. All words fall into one of two categories—words that conform to God's words and words which do not. One good way to generate disobedient words is to talk a lot. "In the multitude of words sin is not lacking, but he who restrains his lips is wise" (Prov. 10:19; cf. 17:27).

Another way is to speak hastily. Ready, fire, aim! One man reports on how he understands the situation. But because he is a fool, the information he passes on is untrustworthy. "A fool has no delight in understanding, but in expressing his own heart" (Prov. 18:2).

Another man has an axe to grind. He is spiteful and puts the worst construction possible on the situation. A third, a liar, listens eagerly. "An evildoer gives heed to false lips; a liar listens eagerly to a spiteful tongue" (Prov. 17:4). And of course, when people rebel against God through talebearing, it is not difficult for them to find a market for their wares. "The words of a talebearer are like tasty trifles, and they go down into the inmost body" (Prov. 18:8; 26:22).

Boys must be taught by judicious example—hearing, waiting, weighing, considering, verifying, and acting according to Scripture. In the biblical home, these standards must be commonplace, and we must expect that we will hold one another accountable. And in particular, fathers must hold their sons accountable. Do not follow common worldly standards in dealing with problems.

"Do you see a man hasty in his words? There is more hope for a fool than for him" (Prov. 29:20). The Bible tells us to be quick to listen, slow to speak. Those who disobey are worse off than a fool. Because they are quick, they may believe themselves to be wise. But biblically the two are not the same.

CHAPTER SEVEN

Laziness and Hard Labor

Taking one thing with another, boys tend to be lazy. This means that one of the central duties parents have with regard to their boys is the duty of teaching and instilling what used to be called a work ethic. "He that gathereth in summer is a wise son: but he that sleepeth in harvest is a son that causeth shame" (Prov. 10:5). The son who causes shame is one who causes shame to his *parents*. The shame is theirs because the responsibility to teach the lessons of work was theirs.

Work is not a result of the fall of Adam, but work goes the difficult way it does because of the fall. Prior to the advent of sin in the world, Adam was given the task of tending the garden and naming the animals. We were created for work. But when sin entered, God in His wisdom saw that thorns and thistles were now needed (Gen. 3:17–19). In His *grace*, God cursed the ground. Just as the law is a schoolmaster to bring us to Christ, so is the sweat of the brow. Sinners don't do well living on the Big Rock Candy Mountain.

And so this is why boys need to be taught and disciplined in *physical* labor. Of course it is not an end in itself—the point should always be grace—but in the hands of wise parents, hard physical work is an important part of a boy's discipleship. He needs to know what it is like to be exhausted, to have calluses on his hands, and to work when his body does not really want to anymore. He needs this; God said so. He is a son of Adam.

In dealing with all these issues, a boy learns to distinguish between the ever-popular notions of self-*esteem*, and the biblical concept of self-*respect*. Self-esteem is found in Galatians 6:3. "For if a man think himself to be something, when he is nothing, he deceiveth himself." A boy lounging on a soft couch can fancy himself quite the working man. But self-*respect* is found in the next verse. "But let every man prove his own work, and then shall he have rejoicing in himself alone, and not in another. For every man shall bear his own burden" (vv. 4–5). Work should not just be done, it should be proven, tested. And when it is, a boy learns the deep and godly satisfaction that comes from a job well done.

Parental Preparation

A boy who learns to settle into his laziness is being prepared by his parents for a life of *frustration*. "The soul of the sluggard desireth, and hath nothing: but the soul of the diligent shall be made fat" (Prov. 13:4). Nothing ever seems to go right for him; the breaks always go to the other guy. The ball always bounces away from him. He is adept at making excuses, and so he continues to do so—but this does not make the frustration go away. Frustration in the hands of a spin doctor is still frustration. Why is the other guy always so "lucky?" The answer is that everything comes to the one who hustles while he waits.

A boy who is allowed to drift downward into this sin is also being prepared for a life of poverty.

> Go to the ant, thou sluggard; consider her ways, and be wise: which having no guide, overseer, or ruler, provideth her meat in the summer, and gathereth her food in the harvest. How long wilt thou sleep, O sluggard? When wilt thou arise out of thy sleep? Yet a little sleep, a little slumber, a little folding of the hands to sleep: so shall thy poverty come as one that travelleth, and thy want as an armed man. (Prov. 6:6–11)

God does not just promise poverty to this young man; He promises that it will come upon him like a thug with a gun. In the good providence of God, the lazy man is not going to be treated with tenderness. Parents who allow this pattern to develop while their son is under their oversight are asking the providential hand of God to work him over with a baseball bat.

In addition, parents who allow their son to neglect work are trying to arrange a rotten reputation for him. "As vinegar to the teeth, and as smoke to the eyes, so is the sluggard to them that send him" (Prov. 10:26). When employers are irritated to this extent, they do not keep their opinions to themselves—nor should they. When someone fills out a negative job evaluation, or tells a prospective new employer that Billy here needs to learn what "get the lead out" means, he is *not* gossiping. Work is a public activity and should be publicly evaluated. A boy steeped in laziness will be evaluated roughly, and should be.

And last, parents who rob their sons of a work ethic have taken from him one of this life's most precious gifts—sabbath rest. The fourth commandment has two parts, and they depend upon one another. One part, of course, is the day of rest, but the other part is the six days of labor. Without the labor, the rest is nonsensical. Without the rest, the work is slavery. Learned together, a boy comes to comprehend the dignity of labor that is offered up to God in the name of Christ. He learns to rest on the first day of the week in a way that consecrates all his subsequent labors.

So much of this runs contrary to the way the carnal mind thinks we might come to believe it is impossible. And it *is* impossible, apart from the gospel of Christ. This is why the discipline of work should be imparted to a boy along with careful teaching on the meaning of the cross of Jesus Christ. This is because the foundation of a biblical work ethic is a biblical grace ethic.

In the end, laziness is intended by God to be an object lesson. This means that other mothers get to point at *your* son in order to warn their boys not to be like that. As my grandmother once put it to her six sons, "Be good. Don't be like other boys." "I went by the field of the lazy man, and by the vineyard of the man devoid of understanding" (Prov. 24:30). The results of laziness are obvious for all to see, and they *should* be pointed out. Diligent parents use lazy boys in the community as a negative object lesson, and they labor to keep their own sons from being used by other parents the same way.

Disgrace of Laziness

However common it is, the Bible teaches that laziness remains a disgrace. "He who has a slack hand becomes poor, but the hand of the diligent makes rich. He who gathers in summer is a wise son; he who sleeps in harvest is a son who causes shame" (Prov. 10:4–5). As a sin which brings shame, we should consider well some of its identifying characteristics. As we learn this, we should remember that laziness has an obvious alternative. "Go to the ant, you sluggard!" (Prov. 6:6–11). For boys, repetition at this point is necessary.

No continuity: Laziness has no follow-through. A lazy boy may have bursts of activity, and he may even get something done during one of them. But he does not maintain; he does not persevere. "The lazy man does not roast what he took in hunting, but diligence is man's precious possession" (Prov. 12:27). Sometimes the lack of follow-through is extraordinary—a very simple thing could be done to bring a project to completion, but he does not do it. "A lazy man buries his hand in the bowl, and will not so much as bring it to his mouth again. Strike a scoffer, and the simple will become wary; rebuke one who has understanding, and he will discern knowledge" (Prov. 19:24–25). The solution to laziness is seen in this passage as well—the lazy boy must be permitted to eat his own cooking. His parents must not subsidize him in it.

Excuses: This is hard to avoid because laziness is full of excuses. "The lazy man says, There is a lion outside! I shall be slain in the streets!" (Prov. 22:13). Sometimes the excuses are unreasonable—the ancient Hebrew equivalent of "the dog ate my homework," or "aliens kidnapped me— what year is it?" Other times the excuses may seem more reasonable, but the results are still the same.

In order to work well, *preparations* to work well are necessary. A lazy boy promises himself that he will get to work when the time comes, at the last minute. He has great (hypothetical) plans. But when the time for work comes, he discovers that some preliminary work was apparently necessary. So now he has a *new* excuse, but the age of the excuse does not alter the outcome. "The sluggard will not plow by reason of the cold; therefore shall he beg in harvest, and have nothing" (Prov. 20:4). However reasonable the excuse may appear in his own eyes, he still has nothing.

Foolishness: Laziness is full of purported "wisdom." "In all labor there is profit, but idle chatter leads only to poverty. The crown of the wise is their riches, but the foolishness of fools is folly" (Prov. 14:23–24). The lazy man wears his foolish talk *like a crown*. He may be full of proverbial wisdom concerning work, but his wisdom is like the legs of a lame man (Prov. 26:7).

"The lazy man says, 'There is a lion in the road! A fierce lion is in the streets!' As a door turns on its hinges, so does the lazy man on his bed. The lazy man buries his hand in the bowl; it wearies him to bring it back to his mouth. The lazy man is wiser in his own eyes than seven men who can answer sensibly" (Prov. 26:13–17). Even though the lifestyle is ludicrous, and the folly is apparent to all around, the lazy man has it all figured out. He has more wisdom (in his own eyes) than seven wise men.

Irritation: Of course, laziness is an irritation to others. This is why it leads to conflicts in the home. "As vinegar to the teeth and smoke to the eyes, so is the lazy man to those who send him" (Prov. 10:26). This is not surprising. If one of them is lazy, two men will have very different ideas of what constitutes diligence.

Compounding: Laziness compounds with interest. "Laziness casts one into a deep sleep, and an idle person will suffer hunger" (Prov. 19:15). "The soul of a lazy man desires, and has nothing; but the soul of the diligent shall be made rich" (Prov. 13:4). Laziness is not rest; it does not prepare for work. It only prepares for more laziness. The laziness *grows*, along with frustrated desire.

Laziness to Deceit

The most noticeable aspect of laziness is its connection to hastiness and then deceit. "The plans of the diligent lead surely to plenty, but those of everyone who is hasty, surely to poverty. Getting treasures by a lying tongue is the fleeting fantasy of those who seek death" (Prov. 21:5–6). Laziness is a set up for boneheadedness and lies.

The problem of dishonesty in work and labor is a difficult one to address because it is often the case that the first one "lied to" is the liar himself. He is dishonest in his work and labor, and in order to do this most effectively, he must be dishonest first with himself. A young man must be taught that the truth about himself is not seen by looking into his own heart; the truth is found by looking into the mirror of the Word (Jas. 1:24–25). The Word of God is the *only* solution to self-deception.

With that understanding, he should know that honest work belongs to the Lord. "Honest weights and scales are the Lord's; all the weights in the bag are *His* work" (Prov. 16:11). The Lord identifies with honest work. The weights in the bag are His; the nails in the wall are His; the repair job is His—provided it is done honestly. The honest report on homework is His.

But the lure of dishonesty is still strong. If God identifies with honest work, and honest business, then why is there any problem? We live in a fallen world. Sin is attractive, at least at the beginning. "Bread gained by deceit is sweet to a man, but afterward his mouth will be filled with gravel" (Prov. 20:17). Learning honesty means learning to taste the gravel early. Discipline of dishonesty in boys is consequently very important. The simple do not learn this, and listen to the call of a foolish woman. "'Whoever is simple, let him turn in here; and as for him who lacks understanding, she says to him, 'Stolen water is sweet, and bread eaten in secret is pleasant.' But he does not know that the dead are there, that her guests are in the depths of hell" (Prov. 9:16–18). Again, there is a sweetness at the beginning of dishonesty and deception, but the end is a calamity. Often people learn how "sweet" it is to be dishonest in early life, in their school work, but the end is hell.

It should be obvious by now that laziness is *hard*. "The way of the lazy man is like a hedge of thorns, but the way of the upright is a highway" (Prov. 15:19). Proverbs teaches us that laziness is counterproductive; it does not accomplish its desired end. "The hand of the diligent will rule, but the lazy man will be put to forced labor" (Prov. 12:24).

CHAPTER EIGHT

Money Paths and Traps

The sanctification of the checkbook is extraordinarily difficult for many. We like to tell ourselves that obedience to God's way is "impractical," as though we knew more about it than He does. Always, always, we must turn to the Word. And on this subject, we have a treasury of doctrine and it is a treasury that should be opened for our sons.

Wealth is good. We see this when wisdom promises her blessings: "That I may cause those who love me to inherit wealth, that I may fill their treasuries" (Prov. 8:21; cf. v. 18). When we obey God, as a general rule, we may expect His blessings, financial blessings included. "The blessing of the LORD makes one rich, and He adds no sorrow with it" (Prov. 10:22).

This means that wealth must be sought God's way. As we teach our sons to seek God's blessings upon their endeavors, we must teach them to do what He says to do. What does God say to do with regard to the acquisition of wealth? First He says to fear Him—"By humility and the fear of the LORD are riches and honor and life" (Prov. 22:4). A second principle is that we must be generous—"The generous soul will be made rich, and he who waters will also be watered himself" (Prov. 11:25; cf. 22:9; 28:27; 11:24). We have already discussed the third principle in detail, which is to bring up sons who know how to work hard: "In all labor there is profit, but idle chatter leads only to poverty" (Prov. 14:23).

A young man has to be taught the importance of savings. True wisdom knows how to defer gratification and provides for others downstream. Our culture is truly rebellious at this point. "A good man leaves an inheritance to his children's children, but the wealth of the sinner is stored up for the righteous" (Prov. 13:22). Related to this, young men need to be taught to be wary of borrowing. This is because although borrowing is not an evil activity in itself it does reveal an order of dominion. Borrowing is an indication of servitude—"The rich rules over the poor, and the borrower is servant to the lender" (Prov. 22:7). But the activity of lending itself is blessed. "He who has pity on the poor lends to the LORD, and He will pay back what he has given" (Prov. 19:17).

A young man also has to learn financial perspective. Nothing is more unseemly than a thirteen-year-old with a briefcase who wants to be rich someday. Financial balance is determined by the Word of God, and that alone.

What is more important than wealth? Sons must learn that salvation is more important. "Riches do not profit in the day of wrath, but righteousness delivers from death" (Prov. 11:4). Integrity is far more important. "Better is the poor who walks in his integrity than one perverse in his ways, though he be rich" (Prov. 28:6). A sensible woman is worth far more than wealth—"Houses and riches are an inheritance from fathers, but a prudent wife is from the LORD" (Prov. 19:14). A young man should value his honor and reputation. "A good name is to be chosen rather than great riches, loving favor rather than silver and gold" (Prov. 22:1). And of course, the Scriptures put a great value on low blood pressure —"Do not overwork to be rich; because of your own understanding, cease!" (Prov. 23:4).

> Do not let your heart envy sinners, but be zealous for the fear of the Lord all the day; for surely there is a hereafter, and your hope will not be cut off. Hear, my son, and be wise; and guide your heart in the way.

Do not mix with winebibbers, or with gluttonous eaters of meat; for the drunkard and the glutton will come to poverty, and drowsiness will clothe a man with rags. (Prov. 23:17–21)

Throwing it Away

We may be induced to throw our money away in any number of ways. For young men, at the head of the list are the ways they lose money through the sensual snares which await them. Typically when such sins are mentioned, it is so that God's people will know that they are bad. This is of course true, but a much more limited point is that they are *expensive.*

Boys are in tune with their appetites, and therein lies a problem. "The righteous eats to the satisfying of his soul, but the stomach of the wicked shall be in want" (Prov. 13:25). Both the righteous and the wicked have a stomach and an appetite. But the righteous can eat and be satisfied, while the wicked are driven by an appetite which is out of control. In any of these areas, the issue is generally not the thing being considered, i.e., sleep, sex, etc., but rather whether or not God's law is honored, and whether or not self-control is in evidence.

Luxury: "Luxury is not fitting for a fool, much less for a servant to rule over princes" (Prov. 19:10). Luxurious display is inappropriate for a fool, that is, a fool should not have it. And if he does get it, he won't have it for long. The fool thinks, "If only . . . If only I could get that nice of a car, if only I could get those expensive clothes, if only I could get that wonderful food." But it is not fitting.

Frivolity: Boys throw a lot of money away through frivolity. "He who tills his land will have plenty of bread, but he who follows frivolity will have poverty enough! A faithful man will abound with blessings, but he who hastens to be rich will not go unpunished. To show partiality is not good, because for a piece of bread a man will transgress. A man with an evil eye hastens after riches, and does not consider that poverty will come upon him" (Prov. 28:19–22). A number of issues are addressed in this passage—trying to get rich quickly, showing favoritism, miserliness—but the warning presented first is against frivolity. The Hebrew can mean either frivolity and vanity, or frivolous and empty fellows. The contrast is with one who tills his land, so the meaning is apparently referring to one who follows vain and pleasurable pursuits instead of working. What he chases after may have the appearance of work or not—but it comes up empty. Just to keep this from becoming too abstract, one common frivolous use of time and money is spending a weekend watching videos.

Gluttony: Gluttony in Scripture does *not* refer to someone having a second helping of the mashed potatoes. Rather it refers to the sensualist—the drunkard of food. Scripturally, the glutton is a "riotous eater." For example, the ancient Romans had rooms called *vomitoria* where guests could prepare themselves for the "second course." This kind of sensual pursuit of food leads to poverty.

"He who loves pleasure will be a poor man; he who loves wine and oil will not be rich" (Prov. 21:17). The issue is not the pleasure, but rather the inordinate love of it. What the foolish man loves (sensual experience), he winds up losing. "There is desirable treasure, and oil in the dwelling of the wise, but a foolish man squanders it" (Prov. 21:20).

Sleep: Sleep is another good sensual way to lose money. This is obviously connected to the sin of laziness discussed earlier. But the love of sleep needs to be mentioned here as well. "Do not love sleep, lest you come to poverty; open your eyes, and you will be satisfied with bread" (Prov. 20:13). And incidentally, a good way for young men to learn bad sleeping habits is for them to stay up until one thirty in the morning watching the stupid videos they rented earlier in this section.

Sex: And of course, there is sex. When Solomon warns his son against the loose woman, he connects this warning: "Lest aliens be filled with your wealth, and your labors go to the house of a foreigner" (Prov. 5:10). "For by means of a harlot a man is reduced to a crust of bread; and an adulteress will prey upon his precious life" (Prov. 6:26). The economic consequences of immorality are *not* tiny. "Whoever loves wisdom makes his father rejoice, but a companion of harlots wastes his wealth" (Prov. 29:3). The reason there is so much porn on the net is that there are thousands of fools with credit cards who want to pay money for flickering images on a screen. The truism that a fool and his money are soon parted has been taken into the big leagues.

Dishonesty: As with laziness, dishonesty frequently appears in the concerns of money: "Diverse weights and diverse measures, they are both alike, an abomination to the Lord" (Prov. 20:10). The word *abomination* here refers to something disgustingly wicked. This particular sin is right in there, in God's sight, with sodomy (Lev. 18:22), bowing down to idols (Deut. 7:25), or witchcraft (Deut. 18:12). "Diverse weights are an abomination to the Lord, and dishonest scales are not good" (Prov. 20:23). A dishonest man is therefore a wicked man. "The wicked man does deceptive work, but he who sows righteousness will have a sure reward" (Prov. 11:18). A dishonest boy is seeking to grow up into a dishonest man.

Dishonesty frequently involves *tomorrow.* "Do not boast about tomorrow, for you do not know what a day may bring forth. Let another man praise you, and not your own mouth; a stranger, and not your own lips" (Prov. 27:1–2). Not completing work on time is dishonesty. Not completing it on time with the quality promised is dishonesty. If a son promised to mow a neighbor's yard this next Saturday, but doesn't get to it for three weeks, and no arrangements are made, then the problem is one of dishonesty.

Not surprisingly, dishonesty brags. The fact that so many boys brag inordinately should be a tip-off. "Whoever falsely boasts of giving is like clouds and wind without rain" (Prov. 25:14). Although this is a proverb concerning claims of generosity, we may apply to other forms of "giving" as well. This young man is all hat and no cattle, all foam and no beer. He is clouds and wind without rain, all halo and no saint. People boast vainly of how much they will give, how much they will earn, how much they will do, how much they will accomplish. But when we come to count it up, not much is there.

Dishonesty frequently begins at home. It is almost always *learned* there. "Whoever robs his father or his mother, and says, 'It is no transgression,' the same is companion to a destroyer" (Prov. 28:24). And this is the worst form of dishonesty because it is perpetrated against loved ones, but is often excused, as here, because it is "all in the family."

A son should have two kinds of work assigned to him in the home. The first can be categorized as the son learning to pull his fair share—chores, in other words. Everyone in the family has certain things to do, and they do them.

But a son should also have additional work assigned to him, and he should be paid for it. With the pay comes the requirement that he learn to manage that pay (along with his allowance) in line with the Scriptures. This work should be sufficient for a steady income. When a boy is old enough to get a job outside the home all the same principles apply.

A father should teach his son to manage a checkbook, to tithe, to save, to be generous, and lastly, to spend. He grows up to be a worshiper with his money first and a consumer last. When he earns one hundred dollars (for example), he must tithe ten dollars. For the rest, he should be required to put twenty dollars into savings, set aside twenty for generosity to others—birthday gifts, buying pizza for the guys—and he can use the remainder on his needs. The lessons learned here can begin very early. My two-year-old grandson is given ten cents in the evening before bed. He carefully counts it out, sets aside the tithe of a penny, and then puts seven cents in the offering on the Lord's Day. In all this, the same principles we have seen earlier apply. A boy grows up to do what he learned to do as a boy.

CHAPTER NINE

Christian Liberty

For multiple reasons, certain "ethical standards" which used to be taken for granted in the Christian world are no longer. In some ways this is good and represents a rejection of various extra-biblical legalisms. But in other ways this phenomenon has been the result of Christians being affected by the moral confusions of our surrounding culture. Recent years have seen terrible erosion in our ability to distinguish good from evil; in certain frightening ways, the ethical competence of the Christian world is frankly disintegrating.

In some places, the standards have simply collapsed. This is nothing other than old-fashioned backsliding and is fairly common in our modern evangelical circles. But in the midst of this general ethical slide, another pattern has appeared as well, one where the banner of Christian liberty is being waived in favor of certain practices that would once have been rejected out of hand. Many Christians now enjoy a glass of wine at dinner, or smoke cigars or pipes, as a genuine exercise of their Christian liberty. So far, so good, as the sage put it. But enter the problem: teenaged boys like liberty because they need something to swing around on the end of a rope. In this climate, it is not long before some young men are pushing the limits of liberty, or they are exercising their liberties without charity.

As we begin this discussion, we must start where all discussions of convoluted subjects should start, which is to say, with definitions. Once we have defined the phrase

"Christian liberty," we may then proceed to applications.

One classic statement of the meaning of Christian liberty is found in one of the great Reformation confessions formulated at Westminster (WCF 20). While *Christian liberty* is a fine-sounding phrase, and it rolls easily off the tongue, our fathers in the faith were not as enamored of slogans as we are and have dealt thoroughly with the deeper ramifications of all this. We should be careful to follow their example when we ask, "What should we mean, exactly, by Christian liberty?"

In the first place, liberty in Christ means freedom from guilt, God's judgment, and the condemnation of moral law. It also means we are delivered *from* the wickedness of the world, the hatred of Satan, and the dominion of sin. We are also freed from the consequences of such things—afflictions, fear of death, the dominion of death, and Hell. We are also freed *to* certain things—we are free to approach God, and free to obey Him from love, not from fear. But liberty always implies a standard, and this standard always brings with it an antithesis. This means that he who says "free from" must also assert a specified "free to." A man cannot turn away from something without simultaneously turning to something. Liberty always assumes an appeal to law.

With this understood, we can assert that because God is our Lord, He *alone* is Lord of the conscience. This means that, in matters of faith and worship, men cannot command us in His name when He has not spoken. Obedience to men is certainly permissible, but we are prohibited from obeying men as though they had the right to bind the conscience in the same way that God does. We may drive on the right side the road, for example, but we may not do so as a matter of conscience. We can easily acknowledge that godly Christians in the UK are to drive on the left side. These sorts of things are societal house rules and do not bind the conscience. The conscience is bound to respect the existing authorities, as the Bible teaches, but there is nothing essentially moral about the right side of the road. Mere men, on their own authority, have no authority whatever to bind the conscience.

Now this leads us to the issues which frequently trouble us—what do you say when your son wants to smoke cigars? And you do not mind cigars, but the thought of your seventeen-year-old smoking one is troublesome, or comic, or both. And suppose he is asking in the name of Christian liberty? "Dad, we left that fundamentalist church five *years* ago!"

The end or purpose of Christian liberty is not to smoke or drink; liberty is given for the pursuit of holiness. Those who wave the banner of Christian liberty so that they might do whatever they might want to do *have not understood the doctrine at all*. The point is not to drink or smoke or dance according to our own whims, in the light of our own wisdom, but to do whatever we do before the Lord, with the increase of joy and holiness obvious to all. Our guide on how this is to be done is the *Bible*, and not our pet evangelical traditions. And this is why the mature may drink wine to the glory of God, and the same *cannot* be applied to young men who may be more concerned about looking cool than being holy.

The issue of authority is also relevant. Not surprisingly, false claims to liberty frequently collide with authority. As boys grow older, they are confident that they can "handle" many things. Among those things which they can handle are some dubious activities which their parents disapprove of. A wise son is one who trusts his parents at such points, and who does not chafe under their judgment calls. But teenaged boys, as is well-known, tend to think they are bulletproof, and they take their notions of this invincibility into the moral realm. This leaves them with questionable desires and resistance to that parental authority which questions them.

As mentioned above, all such questions require a judgment call. The Bible nowhere says, "Thou shalt not smoke any form of tobacco while a teen." So who makes the call? And by what standard?

We have to begin by distinguishing moral legislations and moral applications. Of course mere men do not have the authority to declare anything, on their own authority, to be good or evil. So how can we address anything that the Bible does not mention by name? The answer is that the Bible explicitly requires us to make moral judgment calls.

For example, the Bible says that a bishop has to be "of good behavior" (1 Tim. 3:2). He has to have a good reputation with outsiders (v. 7). He must be blameless (v. 2). Now the Bible nowhere tells us whether the gentleman being considered in the next elder election meets these qualifications or not. The Bible describes the qualifications and expects us to get to know that man and then make a judgment call. We have the same kind of situation with this sort of liberty issue.

> But strong meat belongeth to them that are of full age, even those who by reason of use have their senses exercised to discern both good and evil. (Heb. 5:14)

Those who are mature, those who are of full age, those who have been around the block a few times, have had the opportunity *for a lot of ethical practice*. When they have taken advantage of this opportunity, their senses are exercised to be able to discern good from evil. Now clearly, this does not mean that mature Christians are able to tell that murder is wrong, while nobody else knows this. All men have a certain ethical sense planted in them by God, even though unbelievers do suppress a good deal of what God has given to them. And all Christians have the law of God written on their hearts. Every believer has an immediate knowledge of certain ethical distinctions. In fact, this is one of the evidences of true conversion. A new believer instinctively shrinks away from practices which used to be normal for him. "Whosoever abideth in him sinneth not: whosoever sinneth hath not seen him, neither known him" (1 Jn. 3:6).

But there is another category of ethical judgment calls which can only be made by the experienced and mature, those who have given themselves over to the exercise of distinguishing good from evil. This experience is essential when we come to the areas of ethical application when judgment calls are necessary. When we need judgment calls, we should look to those who are experienced in the Word of God, and experienced in this fallen world. And this is why parents are given to sons.

But parents need to exercise their authority here wisely and with caution. If parents simply slap their own personal prejudices down as the law, it will not take long for their son to see through it. But if they establish the central principle of Christian liberty and require particular applications of this principle in all wisdom, the situation will be quite different.

> For, brethren, ye have been called unto liberty; only use not liberty for an occasion to the flesh, but by love serve one another. (Gal. 5:13)

What is liberty *for*? It is given so that we might serve one another in love. It is not given as an occasion for the flesh. Young men rarely agitate for their liberties while serving others in love. They are usually after their own jollies, tinglies, and whatnot.

> For so is the will of God, that with well doing ye may put to silence the ignorance of foolish men: As free, and not using your liberty for a cloke of maliciousness, but as the servants of God. (1 Pet. 2:15–16)

When a son *demands* his liberties in a self-seeking way, you can rest assured that someone else is going to be harmed. We are called to live *as free*; the use of true Christian liberty threatens no one. But when people clutch at self-centeredness in the name of liberty, the thing is a cloak for malice.

While they promise them liberty, they themselves
are the servants of corruption: for of whom a man
is overcome, of the same is he brought in bondage.
(2 Pet. 2:19)

Christian liberty is given so that we might learn to be
holy. "That he would grant unto us, that we being delivered
out of the hand of our enemies might serve him without
fear, in holiness and righteousness before him, all the days
of our life" (Lk. 1:74–75). When a son asks to able to do
this or that, a very reasonable question is *why?* And when
these "debatable matters" are under discussion and lead to
pointed questions, the answer is almost never, "Because I
want to be holy."

Young men must learn where their temptations will be.
It is not enough to learn what the Bible says about the *content* of our liberty. The Bible is equally emphatic about the
purpose of our liberty. It is very easy to take this wonderful
gift and offer it up on the altar of self. In other words, the
attitude becomes, "I get to do this, and you can't find a Bible
verse to make me stop." But this misses the point of the gift
and disobeys Paul's injunction stated earlier (Gal. 5:13).

Paul teaches in Romans 6:18–23 that freedom from sin
necessarily entails slavery to righteousness (v. 18). If we are
not serving God as slaves, bearing fruit to holiness (v. 22),
then this means we do not comprehend the point of Christian liberty. There are really only two alternatives—if we are
not growing in grace and true personal holiness then anything we do is an act of slavery—not liberty. Rather, we are
slaves to sin, and it does not matter if as "slaves to sin" we
smoke a cigar or not, or drink beer or not. In other words,
we must never think that a class of "behaviors" opens up
to anyone apart from personal holiness. There is no middle
territory between the two.

Christian liberty is nothing other than slavery to God.
The only alternative to this is slavery to man and his desires,
and this includes the young man in question and his desires.

But with all this said, wine *was* given to gladden the heart of man (Ps. 104:15), and one of the duties a father has is that of teaching his son to drink.

CHAPTER TEN

Mom and Sisters

An important task for husbands and fathers is teaching mothers about sons. Husbands and wives are in fact different from one another, and one clear fruit of this difference is yet more differences—the differences between their sons and daughters. After this, things rapidly become even more complicated. We have, obviously, in the first rank, father/son and father/daughter relationships, as well as mother/son and mother/daughter relationships. But then at the second tier we find brother/sister relationships, followed closely by brother/brother and sister/sister. Add to the mix any complications resulting from pluralities—two sons, one daughter, or four daughters and one son, that sort of thing.

As the head of the home, the father is responsible to know the spiritual state of the home, how each member is doing in his relationship with God, and how they are all doing with one another. A father needs to know the state of his flock (Prov. 27:23). If we walk in the light, as God is in the light, we have fellowship with one another (1 Jn. 1:7). If we are not in fellowship with one another, then (at the least) one person is not in fellowship with God. But while the *fact* of any strained relationships may be easy for a husband and father to ascertain, the underlying causes of the temptations may be much more difficult for him to identify.

Principles for Moms

So considerable wisdom is required in all this, and a good part of the task lies in teaching a wife how to understand her sons. Related to this, a man must also teach his sons about their *future* wives through teaching them to honor their mothers now. For the moment, let's limit ourselves to the first question. What principles should a man teach his wife about her sons?

The first is the need for a mother to blend the apparent contraries of *respect* and *toughness*. Mothers with a critical or harsh spirit certainly can be hard on their sons, but it is a demeaning and emasculating hardness. And at the other end of the spectrum, mothers can be respectful of their sons in such a way that they never require anything of them. This kind of respect deteriorates rapidly into a mollycoddling mess. But a mother who approaches her son with wisdom is one who *respects* and consequently *expects*. "Of course you can do this, son. It's the right thing to do." And when a wise mother sees insecurity in her son, the response should not be scorn, it should not be sympathy. The right response is *respect*. Boys can rise to respect, when they might crater under harsh pressure or puff up in response to excessive praise.

Another important principle is that of seeing small boys as future men. The way boys learn to deal with their various immature "passions" will generally be the way they deal with adult passions. A boy who is not obviously learning self-control with regard to his temper, his stomach, his video games, or his school work is a boy who will *still* lack self-control when sexual temptation arrives. Many times mothers unwittingly train boys to mistreat their future wives through sinful indulgence of boyish passions. It is important to distinguish here between the godly service a mother is supposed to supply the household (like cooking the meals) and an ungodly catering that will help destroy her son (like cooking a second breakfast when her son gets up three hours after everyone else, and for no good reason).

A third principle for a mother to learn is that when a godly father is disciplining a boy, he is doing so while *remembering*. He used to think the way his son thinks; he used to receive what his son is now receiving; he used to connive the way his son is conniving. A mother can and should discipline her son, but she cannot do it while *remembering*. She therefore needs her husband's perspective in order to *aim* the way she ought. For her to have his perspective, he must talk about it with her, and not just assume that everyone in the world has the same memories and experiences he has.

Fourth, a mother needs to realize that when she gets exasperated or annoyed with her sons, she is helping them to learn how to control or manipulate her. The drill usually goes like this: A son doesn't do what he was asked to do seven or eight times. Mom finally gets steamed and flares up over it. Mom has more of a tender conscience about her annoyance than son does about his disobedience. She consequently apologizes, he magnanimously forgives her, and the quarter ends with him two touchdowns and a field goal ahead. The solution is for her to cheerfully require obedience from her sons long before annoyance is even a possibility.

And last, a wise mother knows that God has given her to her sons, and her sons to her, and that when the gift is received with wisdom, the blessings are tremendous and flow in both directions. But if the relation is foolishly embraced, the book of Proverbs poignantly prophecies a coming maternal grief.

Keeping the Difference

As parents bring up their children in the nurture and admonition of the Lord, the ethics of childrearing remain constant. But the differences between the sexes require that parents govern their children with wisdom. Not only are these children different from one another, these differences reflect the wisdom of God, who intends for them to serve Him differently.

The purpose here is to outline some of the common pitfalls which face mothers as they deal with their sons. Of course, the father has the responsibility to see to it that the relationship between his wife and his sons is what it ought to be. Nevertheless, trouble often arises between mother and son which he needs to be aware of. Sometimes this trouble is visible to a mother, and sometimes it is not. Boys need to get knocked down. The first "blows" they receive should be right at home during their first several years of existence and delivered by those who know and love them best. This is the time when parents must establish the lines of authority, and the father must see to it that the boy's mother is respected and honored by him. Unless this is done when the boy is two to four years old, the trouble for Mom later on will be considerable.

As the son grows older, and if mother has a hard time maintaining a good relationship with her son through parental discipline, she may attempt to compensate for it through developing an emotional closeness with him. "I know he can be a real pill, but we have had some really good talks. I think he is really opening up to me." What may actually be happening is the son is learning how to manipulate his mother. In other words, if he tells her how his day at school went and talks with her just a *little* bit, a great deal of disobedience and disrespect will be overlooked.

When mothers face this temptation to mollycoddle their sons, they should know that if they give way to it, they are destroying their sons. Any Christian family should, of course, be characterized by kindness and by "good talks," but there is a counterfeit kindness which kills. Emotional closeness or intimacy which ignores sin is not a sign of better things to come; it is an unmarked package ticking ominously.

By the same token, there is a type of toughness in discipline which builds. And we must remember that discipline is not just limited to responses to disobedience and sin on the part of children; discipline also includes patient instruction when the child encounters some of life's ordinary difficulties.

Building Toughness

A family with young sons was once in our home, and in the course of our meal together some hot food hurt one of the boys. Gently, and without any harshness at all, the father stopped his son, who had started to cry, and *taught* him. "What do you do when this happens? You smile and keep on playing." Such lessons, delivered in this fashion, are worth mountains of gold.

This can, of course, be easily misunderstood. No one is saying that a boy with a severed limb should be yelled at for bleeding on the carpet. Nevertheless, instilling toughness in boys is extraordinarily important. A masculine toughness is the only foundation upon which a masculine tenderness may be safely placed. Without a concrete foundation, thoughtfulness, consideration, and sensitivity in men are simply gross. So mothers must take particular care against allowing some of their feminine strengths to be the occasion of stumbling for their sons. Three things are necessary as mothers consider this.

The first is that she should talk regularly with her husband about her sons and her relationship with them. (Of course they should confer about daughters as well, but Mom is receiving something additional in her talks about the boys. She does not initially know how boys think and respond, and her husband does.) Any number of things may be happening which she does not see and concerning which her husband's advice would be invaluable.

Secondly, she must have the respect and obedience of her sons. The older and bigger they get, the more obedient they should be. A son who is a foot and a half taller than his mother should hear her with respect. Of course she should be careful not to issue needless requirements, but when she requires something, it should be cheerfully done. If it is not, then she should immediately involve her husband. The central issue is not the thing to be done, but rather teaching the son to honor his mother, as the commandment says, and to respect women generally.

Third, she must never subsidize her sons' laziness. Masculine inertia is difficult for anyone to deal with, and the aversion which many boys have to academic rigor is renowned. But educational laziness is the mother of poverty and sloth. Whether it involves homework from a Christian school, or the schoolwork supervised at home by a homeschooling mother, the word which should characterize the academic activity of the home is *industry*. Homeschooling mothers, in particular, have to check the work being done against an objective standard. Boys can usually work much harder than they say they can. In all this, under the father's supervision, the mother can equip her sons to rise up and call her blessed.

Making Manners

Another aspect of this is the task of teaching sons how to treat their mothers, and this means instruction in manners. Boys have a need to be respected, but sometimes this need can be communicated in some strange ways. And because boys can gravitate toward such strange forms of communicating their boyhood, they may come to think that manners are for sissies.

A very easy mistake for young boys to make is that of thinking that masculinity consists of being rudely tough, or gross, or both. A ten-year-old boy can readily think that masculinity is displayed whenever he can make all the girls in his class go *eewwwww*. This is of course not the case, but we still have to qualify what we are saying.

There is a fine line here because there *is* a type of boy who is effeminate and displays that effeminacy through being a "well-mannered" and mousy little boy. This arouses the disgust of the surrounding boys who, in a perfect frenzy of metaphor-mixing, proceed to throw out the well-mannered baby with the mousy bathwater.

In addition, those adults who care the most about "manners" often do not understand masculinity either, and so they cannot help boys to make the distinction which they themselves blur. This means that a boy will view all attempts to "teach him manners" as simply an effort by the adult world to make him craven, which he does not want to do. He knows intuitively that a well-mannered boy is *not* a boy who acts like his sister.

Put another way, manners for boys should be a means of disciplining and directing strength, and not a means of denying it. This means that boys need to be taught that manners are a means of showing and receiving honor. Honor is a concept which boys instinctively understand and love, but they still have to be taught to direct it with wisdom. Honor, in its turn, cannot be understood apart from authority and obedience.

As with so many of these things, there is an "intangible" element here. There is an authority which badgers a boy into resentment, and there is an authority which liberates him. A boy might seethe over a mildly cutting remark from his older sister about his dishwasher loading habits, and then the next moment be daydreaming about a drill instructor screaming in his face from a range of about two inches. When men get to telling stories to one another, boot camp stories are frequently in the mix. They rarely tell stories about the time their older sister bossed them around the kitchen.

Boys thrive under authority and are not threatened by it. At the same time, the authority must be of the kind which understands masculinity and nurtures it by hammering it. One of the "hammers" should be a short course in manners.

The heart of masculinity involves the willing assumption of an appropriately assigned responsibility. Manners for boys should be in line with this and not contradict it. Manners for men should therefore point to or illustrate their distinctive responsibilities, and young boys should be in training for this. One of the things we do in our household (common in another era) is that we have the men stand around the dinner table until all the ladies have been seated. This includes vrey young grandsons. When boys are grown, they need to have learned, years before their earliest memory, that men have constant responsibilities and duties with regard to women. Boys should not be allowed to think that manners are something which women impose on men. If they do come to think this, then they will start to react like Huck Finn chafing under the constraints of civilization. Rather, they should see manners as something which men teach boys to do, for the sake of honoring and protecting women, and for the sake of living graciously with them.

With this as a backdrop, a few particulars. A priority should be placed on those manners and customs which place a distinction between men and women. In this class we should put men seating women at the dinner table, opening and holding doors, standing when a woman enters the room, walking on the sidewalk between a woman and the traffic, and so forth.

In a second class would be manners which discipline a young man to think of the comfort and possessions of others—not tipping back in chairs, not putting feet on the coffee table, and not bouncing the basketball next to the china hutch.

A third category would be in the realm of personal presentation: not dressing like a slob, not bolting food, not wearing a baseball cap indoors, etc. In this last category, a boy is being taught, among other things, to present himself as trustworthy in all the categories.

Fundamentally, all these manners are a way of showing honor to others in areas which are not of cosmic importance. At the same time, because they are acts of love, even though they are love in trifles, God considers them important.

Such manners are places where boys are taught to mute their natural energy. Another set of manners are necessary where boys are taught to release that energy. These channels in which aggressiveness can flow should be well-defined and established. We see here the benefits of organized sports and military training. But even on the playing field, "manners" are still important.

When aggressiveness overflows the banks, or when there are no banks, then we have a major problem. And when there is no need for a restraining bank, then things are a lot quieter. But we still have a major problem.

CHAPTER ELEVEN

Church and Worship

In the past, a common taunt against the Christian faith was that "church" was an activity for little old ladies of both sexes. Although this is not heard as often now, for various reasons, we still do not have a good grasp of what masculine piety would *look* like exactly. Feminine piety is generally understood for what it is. But this feminine piety is now considered to be *the* normative form of piety. Whenever masculine piety is displayed (which is rare anymore), we resist it, are deeply concerned about it, or diagnose it as a syndrome needing some increased medication.

Obviously, the Bible does not say that the fruit of the Spirit is love, joy, peace, etc.—*if* you are a man, or *if* you are a woman. The fruit of the Spirit grows and develops in both men and women. At the same time, love, gentleness, and goodness will be manifested differently in different people, depending on their personalities, gifts, station, office, sex, and so forth. Character is a constant—honesty means the same thing whether it is a man or a woman telling the truth. Fidelity is a constant. Avoiding covetousness is always right. The standards of morality do not shift from sex to sex. But the expressions of such things will change according to the situation.

For example, both men and women are told to put on tender mercies. Now feminine piety excels at a certain form of tenderness. But we have taken this feminine giftedness and have made it the norm for all expressions of piety. Masculine piety excels at toughness, but no one usually thinks to include toughness in their catalog of pieties. For example, a young boy who is somewhat timid needs to learn the piety of courage. If he has a good lacrosse coach, he will be urged to knock somebody down to the glory of God. The point is not that boys need to learn courage and that girls do not, but rather that their different callings will affect how that courage is manifested.

Take another example. Suppose a young girl notices that a friend at school seems somewhat discouraged. She asks if anything is wrong and leaves an encouraging note in her friend's locker. She looks her up after school and offers to pray with her. A teacher who sees all this will naturally thank God for this obvious dedication to love and good works. But that same teacher will not readily make this same assumption when he walks by a boy who is slapping a friend on the back of the head, calling him a fathead—even though the boy was doing this because his friend had asked a non-Christian girl out on a date the night before. His zeal for righteousness is not recognized as such.

The disciplines of such piety are first learned in the public worship of God. In order for boys to learn masculine piety in worship we must first make sure we are teaching or inculcating it there. This is problematic for us because so much of modern worship has been thoroughly feminized.

The Church and Femininity

But before proceeding further, an important qualification is necessary. *Masculine worship does not exclude women in the same way that feminine worship excludes men.* Women flourish when men take spiritual responsibility. Men wither or stay away when women lead in the church. So the church is not a men's club—men, women, children and babies gather before the Lord *together*. Masculine worship is not worship for men; it is worship in which men fulfill their responsibilities to *others*. As a result of masculine leadership, women and children are free to contribute to the worship rightly. But they do so because men have taken responsibility. In a scriptural worship service, both masculine and feminine elements will be present, but the masculine will be dominant, in a position of leadership. When the feminine element leads or dominates, the result is that those men who are masculine are encouraged to stay away.

The Church is *corporately* feminine in her relation to Christ as Head. Christ is the bridegroom and the Church is His *bride*. But this feminine relation is covenantal and corporate. A great problem in the Western church has arisen because of the notion that all individual piety must reflect this corporate reality. As Leon Podles has ably shown in *The Church Impotent*, the individualization of piety has meant that individual men must try to learn how to think like a bride. They don't do this very well, and so they stay away. Those who learn to do it well may develop another problem—they may become effeminate. And if they excel, then they become a pencil neck like the Rev. Mr. Kinosling in the *Penrod* stories.

Boys should be able to see masculine leadership throughout the life of the church. From the pulpit, to the session of elders, to the choir, boys should be able to see men they respect. They should not see what is too often the case— missing men or silent men just along for the ride. When men go to church simply to sit in the back, they are teaching their boys to do exactly the same thing, if that.

Such coasting is easy to do, and when it is done long enough, it is even easier to drift away from the faith entirely. This means that little boys should be present in the worship of God early in their lives, and they should receive ongoing training throughout their boyhood. Church should never be "easy" in the sense of requiring no commitment to discipleship.

Worship Itself

So what does the Bible say about nursery, and Sunday School, and keeping the children (*especially* the squirmier boys) with the family during the service? This is something which we all deal with every week. Does the Bible shed light on the subject?

Again, I need to emphasize the difference between principles and methods. It is very easy to fall into the trap of mimicking the externals of anything which we respect. Thus we imitate a friend's hair style and not her charity; a preacher's hand gestures but not his prayer; an educator's textbooks or methods but not his wisdom. This should be a concern in many areas of life, and not surprisingly, it matters here. Remember the parable of the two sons. One said he would go—and did not. The other said he would not—but then did. The second one was obedient (Mt. 21:28–32; cf. 1 Jn. 3:18). Saying you will obey when you won't is a species of lying and hypocrisy; we must guard our hearts against it.

With this in mind, what is our first principle? Children are not to be automatically and routinely excluded from the public worship of God. This is true in both the Old and New Testament. "Blow the trumpet in Zion, consecrate a fast, call a sacred assembly; gather the people, sanctify the congregation, assemble the elders, *gather the children and nursing babes*; let the bridegroom go out from his chamber, and the bride from her dressing room" (Joel 2:16).

In the New Testament, Paul delivers his instruction to the congregations of Ephesus and Colossae in a way which simply assumes the presence of the children. "Children, obey your parents" (Eph. 6:1–3; Col. 3:20). So when the apostle Paul writes to Christian churches, he is not at all reluctant to include the children of that congregation in his exhortations. We also see children routinely included in the life of the saints. "When we had come to the end of those days, we departed and went on our way; and they all accompanied us, *with wives and children*, till we were out of the city. And *we* knelt down on the shore and prayed" (Acts 21:5).

Children, as children, are a very important part of every Christian assembly. They are present with us as we gather before the Lord—they are not just watching us do it. A significant reason many churches keep all their children out of the worship service as a matter of course is that they have bought into the modern pattern of "dumbing down" everything, including the message of salvation, for our children. This is not a biblical assumption. "Justification? My kids aren't ready to hear about that." But the second principle is also important. In the Scriptures, children were not universally included in public worship as a necessary requirement either.

Now all the people gathered together as one man in the open square that was in front of the Water Gate; and they told Ezra the scribe to bring the Book of the Law of Moses, which the LORD had commanded Israel. So Ezra the priest brought the Law before the assembly of men and women *and all who could hear with understanding* on the first day of the seventh month. Then he read from it in the open square that was in front of the Water Gate from morning until midday, before the men and women *and those who could understand*; and the ears of all the people were attentive to the Book of the Law. (Neh. 8:1–3)

And in Exodus 23:17, we see that the "pilgrim festivals" of Israel, held in Jerusalem, required only the males. So there may be times when it is appropriate to have those children who cannot understand back in the nursery. This, when done in wisdom, is not tantamount to excommunication, or a declaration of war on the family. It happened in ancient Israel with some regularity. But the danger here (for us moderns) is that we get used to the convenience of not having to discipline and teach our own children—*that* is being done back in children's church by a wild and zany youth worker—and so our kids grow up with little understanding of how to worship God.

Training for Worship

Boys need oversight and teaching from their fathers in learning how to worship God. It is easy for them to become restless, particularly when the only thing that is expected of them is to sit quietly. A young boy growing up in weekly worship needs to learn how to participate wisely. And there are three things worth mentioning here.

The first is the importance of the Word. "Therefore, laying aside all malice, all deceit, hypocrisy, envy, and all evil speaking, as newborn babes, *desire the pure milk of the word*, that you may grow thereby, if indeed you have tasted that the Lord is gracious" (1 Pet. 2:1–3). God has not left us without direction in how we are to live our lives. This direction is set down for us in a book, which is the Bible. But this is not said so that young men will come to respect and revere the Bible—I am sure that is done already. Parents are involved in the work of teaching and educating their sons, whether at home or at school. They are not doing this because they think it would be "nice" if their sons were educated. They do it because God requires it of them. The reason sons must be educated is that, first, they must be given access to the Word of God (learning how to read), and secondly, they must be taught how to meditate and study (learning how to think about what is read).

So the first thing sons should make sure to do is to work hard and honestly at their school work—even when they do not see the connection between school and the Word of God. There *is* a connection, and if they work hard at their studies, they will one day grow wise enough to see that connection.

Learning to work hard will keep them from coasting. Growing up within the covenant has many great blessings associated with it, and young men must never take those blessings for granted. But it also presents some grand temptations. With regard to the Word, the greatest temptation young men will face from having grown up in the church will be the temptation to assume that they know more than they actually do. Wisdom never comes in a bottle or a can; it must be lived out in a real world.

The sacraments are also important. God has given two sacraments to the church, baptism and the Lord's Supper. The Lord uses both to establish and strengthen *boys* by His grace. A great deal of mischief has been done through a rejection of nourishment available to the saints through the sacraments. Often, young people are kept back from the Lord's Supper because they are not yet spiritually strong. This is refusing to give your son bread when he asks for it—and, being too cheap to give him a stone instead, we give him air. When asked why the bread was refused, the reply is that he wasn't strong enough to eat bread. He was too hungry for food. After he grows up and becomes big and strong, then we can give him bread. With a sort of perverse logic, we starve our children to death, and then point to their subsequent deaths as a good reason for not having fed them.

Let's consider baptism first. "For you are all sons of God through faith in Christ Jesus. For as many of you as were baptized into Christ have put on Christ" (Gal. 3:26–27). Baptism is the mark of God's grace placed on the one who is baptized. Wherever a young man goes, he takes his baptism with him. Whatever he does, he is including his baptism in that action. In baptism, he is dressed in Christ, clothed in Christ. *And wherever he goes, his clothes go.* This means that recalling his baptism in faith will be a source of strength to him. Forgetting it will be a source of chastisement, and an invitation to sin.

Then we must teach our sons the importance of the Lord's Supper—baptism is the door, and the Lord's Supper is the table. A young man does not sit down at the table until he has come through the door. But great blessings are to be found when God's people sit down at the table. "The cup of blessing which we bless, is it not the communion of the blood of Christ? The bread which we break, is it not the communion of the body of Christ?" (1 Cor. 10:16). The Lord's Supper is the mark of God's nourishing grace upon

His saints. Consequently, boys need to be established as communicant saints long before they leave home. One final comment about worship. Music has been one of the chief culprits in the feminization of the church. Many of the "traditional" hymns of the nineteenth century are romantic, flowery, and feminine. (I come, after all, to the garden alone, while the dew is still on the roses.) But the recent rejection of such hymns in favor of contemporary worship music has been a step further away from a biblical masculinity. The current emphasis on "feeling worshipful" is frankly masturbatory, which in men produces a cowardly and effeminate result.

The fact that the church has largely abandoned the singing of psalms means that the church has abandoned a songbook that is thoroughly masculine in its lyrics. The writer of most of the psalms was a warrior, and he knew how to fight the Lord's enemies in song. With regard to the music of our psalms and hymns, we must return to a world of vigorous singing, vibrant anthems, more songs where the tenor carries the melody, open fifths, and glory. Our problem is not that such songs do not exist; our problem is that we have forgotten them. And in forgetting them, we are forgetting our boys. Men need to model such singing for their sons.

CHAPTER TWELVE

Giants, Dragons, and Books

In C. S. Lewis's *The Voyage of the Dawn Treader*, we are given a good example of a boy who was brought up poorly. Eustace Scrubb had stumbled into a dragon's lair, but he did not know what kind of place it was. "Most of us know what we should expect to find in a dragon's lair, but, as I said before, Eustace had read only the wrong books. They had a lot to say about exports and imports and governments and drains, but they were weak on dragons."

It is a standing rebuke for us that there are many Christians who have an open sympathy for the "true" books which Eustace read—full of true facts about governments and drains and exports—and who are suspicious of great works of imagination, like the Narnia stories, or *The Lord of the Rings*, or *Treasure Island*, because they are "fictional," and therefore suspected of lying. The Bible requires us to be truthful above all things, they tell us, and so we should not tell our sons about dragon-fighting. Our sons *need* to be strong on drains and weak on dragons. The irony here is that the Bible, the source of all truth, says a lot about dragons and giants, and very little about drains and exports.

Like Eustace in the dragon lair, we do not recognize our surroundings because we have been reading the wrong kind of books, and this in turn causes us to read the Bible in the wrong way. And then, when the time comes to educate our sons, we stuff their heads with soul-deadening, imagination-killing factoids. But if our sons are to be prepared for the world *God* made, then their imaginations must be fed and nourished with tales about the Red Cross Knight, Jim in the apple barrel, Sam Gamgee carrying Frodo up the mountain, Beowulf tearing off Grendel's arm, and Trumpkin fighting for Aslan while still not believing in him. This type of story is not allowed by Scripture; this type of story is *required* by Scripture. The Bible cannot be read rightly without creating a deep impulse to tell stories which carry the scriptural truth about the kind of war we are in down through the ages.

We fell into sin as a race because we were beguiled by a dragon (Gen. 3:1). God promised to send a warrior who would crush the seed of that serpent (Gen. 3:15), and He has done this in Jesus Christ. In sum, the gospel is the story of a dragon-fight. The serpent of Genesis is the dragon of Revelation (Rev. 20:2), and we are called to rejoice that the dragon has been slain. In contrast, we have reduced the gospel to four basic steps toward personal happiness, and we are much farther from the truth than our fathers were when they told their glorious stories. This is another way of saying that dragon-lore is truer than therapy-speak.

The Bible refers repeatedly to the reality of dragons and winged serpents and indicates that the devil is one of their number. Modern translators are embarrassed by all of this and try to get by with renderings like *jackal* or *crocodile*. They have not gone so far as to translate the words for *dragon* as *export* or *drain*, but they would if they could. The bronze serpent lifted up in the wilderness was a seraph and prefigured the final and complete defeat of Satan, that evil dragon. Our God is a great warrior, and He fights dragons. He calls us to imitate Him in this, and we cannot imitate Him in this without stories of that imitation which fire the imagination.

> Thou didst divide the sea by thy strength: thou brakest the heads of the dragons in the waters. Thou brakest the heads of leviathan in pieces, and gavest

him to meat to the people inhabiting the wilderness. (Ps. 74:13-14)

We see the same kind of thing with giants. Ambrose Bierce once gave a wonderful definition of mythology which we as moderns need to take to heart. He said that mythology was the "body of a primitive people's beliefs concerning its origins, early history, heroes, deities and so forth, as distinguished from the true accounts *which it invents later.*"

With this firmly in mind, the following terms are translated from the Hebrew Old Testament as *gigantes* (giants) in the Septuagint (and occasionally as *titanes*, or titans). First are the Nephilim; the Nephilim proper were the offspring of the sons of God and daughters of men (Gen. 6:1-4). There were giants in the earth then. The Bible also refers to the Rephaim: these were among the original inhabitants of Canaan (Gen. 15:20). They were likely descendants of a certain Repha (1 Chr. 20:4-8). They were also huge. Then we read about the Anakim, who are said to have their descent from the Nephilim (Num. 13:33). The word *gibborim* can be rendered as "mighty men," among whom Nimrod was numbered. Remember also that the Amorites were also giants (Amos 2:9-10). All these terms are used commonly together. In short, Canaan was a land filled with giants. The invasion of Canaan was a war of giant-killing, and a type of the giant-killing Gospel.

Giant-killing is a motif throughout Scripture. In addition to the battles over Canaan, we should note how the war continues through to the end of the Bible. We all know the story of David and Goliath—but it must also be seen as part of a larger, ongoing war on giants (2 Sam. 21:19-22). In the New Testament, Christ bound the strong man: what we find in the life and death of Jesus Christ is *not* an example of a godly giant fighting a puny devil. Rather, Christ became one of *us*, and, as a son of *David*, He bound and defeated the Goliath of that age (Lk. 11:21-22). In this passage from

Luke, Christ takes all the strong man's armor (his *panoply*) and divides the spoil.

The Christian faith is a religion of world conquest. Are the giants who confront us big enough to qualify as giants? And have we taught our sons what they are supposed to do when they grow up? Part of fulfilling the Great Commission involves climbing the beanstalk.

When Israel fought in the Transjordan, the land that would be inherited by Reuben, Gad, and the half tribe of Manasseh, they destroyed both Sihon and Og, the latter of which was certainly a giant. Lest we forget, Scripture reminds us that Og was part of a remnant of the giants. His bed was enormous—king size—but much more was involved than honor. His bed was about thirteen and a half feet by six feet.

It is remarkable how often these two defeated kings come up in Scripture. It happens throughout Deuteronomy (Deut. 1:4; cf. 4:46-47; 29:7; 31:4). Centuries later, under the reign of Solomon, one of the king's officials named Geber is identified as governing the land which Sihon and Og used to have (1 Kgs. 4:19). In the psalms, the psalter of Israel perpetuated the memory of these great battles (Ps. 135:5-12). The next psalm does the same (Ps. 136:18-21). And those Christians who sing the psalms are still singing about it and will do so until the end of the world. After their return from exile, in a great confession of sin, the people recall God's previous kindness in this regard (Neh. 9:22). But what they remembered, many modern Christians want to forget.

When Christians show themselves willing to lose the modern blinders which restrict our reading of the text, we will come to see the Bible as a *fantastic* book, with all the connotations of that word involved. There are many odd places beyond the few cited here in this discussion and many strange things beyond the giants and dragons. And once this happens, we will come to see the duty of training our sons to think this way through the other books they read.

With this said, let's turn to a few particular suggestions. As we do, we will perhaps be accused of recommending escapist literature. This is quite right: we should *want* our sons to escape from all arrogant Enlightenment conceits. Left alone, they will grow up in a modernist dungeon, well-lit with pale green florescent light. If someone comes along and hands them a key that will get them out, someone will warn them, in dire tones. "Careful. Keys are escapist."

And I do not see how I can finish this chapter without being autobiographical. I grew up in Narnia and Archenland and as a boy, considered myself as much an Archenlander as an American. All my sympathies and sentiments were there, and I still cannot read about Shasta's run toward his unknown home without being affected by it. It does no good to tell me that Narnia does not actually exist, because Puddleglum speaks for me here. He would rather live as a free Narnian, even if there is no Narnia, than to acquiesce in the belief that a dank cave was all there was to the world. This was deep loyalty, loyalty in the bones, not neo-orthodoxy. A boy could do far worse than have an allegiance to a nonexistent king. He might grow up, as kids today do, without any loyalties at all. This was not frivolous daydreaming; it was hardheaded realism, and by leading me into these books my father equipped me for things as they really are in this world.

I did not get to Middle Earth until high school, but I saw to it that my children were introduced to *The Lord of the Rings* much earlier than I had been. I would read to the family in the evening, and it was frequently the case that I was not permitted to stop and had to read for three or four hours at a stretch. The first time I read through the trilogy to the kids my son was a two-year-old, and he sat and listened quite patiently. We were not sure how much he was getting, but during the battle scenes, his cheeks would get hot.

Virtues were made *lovely* to me through these stories. Trumpkin did not believe in Aslan, but volunteered to go on a mission that made sense only if Aslan existed. He went because he knew the difference between giving advice and taking orders. "You've had my advice, and now it's the time for orders." And I have known what true faithfulness and loyalty were since then. Too often Christian parents simply seek to make the *rightness* of virtue apparent to their sons. But that is the easy part. The difficulty lies in making virtue altogether lovely, which is what happens in the right kind of story.

Egalitarianism, the political name for carping envy, was made obnoxious, the way it ought to be. The White Witch came upon an extravagant feast at Christmas, with all sorts of waste and conspicuous consumption. "What is the meaning of all this gluttony, this waste, this self-indulgence?" She then turned the party-goers to stone and went on her evil, self-righteous way. We see the White Witch, Judas Iscariot, and federal bureaucrats have a good deal in common—concern for the poor *sincerely* expressed by those who keep the money bag.

Hatred of tyranny in the petty prohibitionisms came the same way. Sam Gamgee comes back to the Shire very different from the thick-fingered peasant that he was when he left. He came back to all kinds of progress, including industry, zoning changes, and a higher level of health consciousness. "'All right, all right,' said Sam. 'That's quite enough. I don't want to hear no more. No welcome, no beer, no smoke, and a lot of rules and orc-talk instead.'" There are some deep lessons for us here—no beer, no smoke, and surgeon-generals all over the place. Saruman was apparently confirmed by our Senate.

In this kind of literature, nobility was stirred up in the small things and was exalted in the great things. When the time came for great deeds, whether the enemy was Smaug, or Sauron, or the Witch, or Long John Silver, or the dragon that St. George killed, these stories were ready to do what Scripture commands us to do. "Finally, brethren, whatsoever things are true, whatsoever things are honest, whatsoever things are just, whatsoever things are pure, whatsoever things are lovely, whatsoever things are of good report; if there be any virtue, and if there be any praise, think on these things" (Phil. 4:8).

Christians are a race of dragon-fighters. Our sons are born to this. Someone ought to tell them.

CHAPTER THIRTEEN

School Work

The lessons of school work are identical to the lessons of work. Every form of honest work is good for a boy, and academic work is not excluded from this. At the same time, the *process* of schooling requires some attention.

Traditional schools pose a particular kind of threat to masculinity. If a school is not careful, they will actively suppress the qualities in their male students which go into the making of a leader. Because of the very nature of institutions, conformity and discipline is of course required. This by itself is not at all a threat to the masculinity of boys—conformity and discipline are also found in the Navy Seals. But in a sexually-integrated school, boys and girls are disciplined together, and frequently the discipline is applied to the older boys by women teachers. In many schools, the entire teaching staff is made up of women. The presence of women teachers is not necessarily a problem, but the absence of male teachers most certainly is. But we have to be careful because the presence of male teachers (in the presence of women) can create another kind of problem for the male students.

Such sexual integration does not create an automatic capitulation to effeminacy, but it most certainly does create a ready occasion for it. Schools with boys and girls together can avoid this problem, but they *cannot* avoid it apart from prayer, study, and discriminating discipline. Put another way, schools which do not think about this problem will *have* this problem in spades.

Boys and Institutional Schools

When boys and girls are disciplined in the same institution, living under the same rules, they respond to it differently, according to their respective natures. The response of the girls is usually far more "friendly" to the concerns of the institution than the response of the boys will be. Put simply, the girls do not color outside the lines. Not surprisingly, the school is pleased and charmed with this response. The boys are not nearly so concerned to please the institution as the girls are. And when girls *are* a problem they are frequently led into that trouble-making status by some of the boys.

This difference between the sexes includes the boys who are not at all rebellious or trouble-making. In a well-disciplined school, the girls respond to the discipline with alacrity, and the boys (who want naturally to put some kind of distance between themselves and the girls) will create that distance by responding willingly, but only so far as is necessary. The guys do what is necessary, but the girls will go the second institutional mile. The guys keep to themselves on their own time while the girls seek out a favorite teacher to have lunch with.

Guys *are* willing to visit with a strong male teacher who is willing to talk with them about hunting, sports, etc. But if there is no teacher of this caliber to talk with, the boys will turn to one another for this outlet. As a friend of mine put it, "Most Christian schools don't hire this kind of man because he probably offended someone in the interview process."

Consequently, in such a school the students who get faculty commendations frequently are the girls and the boys who behave like girls. Now any institution will get more of what it subsidizes and less of what it penalizes. If it acknowledges and rewards boys who act like girls, it will get more of them, much to the disgust of the self-respecting boys. The self-respecting boys include many who are not at all discipline problems, but who are not about to do what it takes to receive the approbation of the school. *That* would require becoming a wuss.

This creates an implicitly adversarial relationship between the school and the godly young men. Because their godliness is masculine, it doesn't fall in line with the goals of the school as readily. Because the masculinity is godly, it does not rebel or disrupt, but merely endures the situation patiently. This too shall pass. And in the meantime, this means that a godly young woman is *far more likely* to be recognized as such by the school than a young man is. Christians who are involved with schools should be diligent in thinking through this issue. Often the lament, "Why are there no godly young men?" should actually be, "Why can't we see them? What is wrong with our institutional eyes?"

When boys are being taught by a staff which is largely composed of women, effeminacy can unwittingly be encouraged. The women expect boys to receive discipline in the same way that the women received it when they were girls. Women teachers need to have a strong biblical definition of masculinity and femininity in their minds, and it helps if there are men on staff who embody the masculinity that we want the boys to grow up into. If this does not happen, the women on staff can be helping to raise a generation of passive manipulators.

In addition, I mentioned above that the presence of male teachers, although it provides young men with a role model, can create its own unique problem. On the up side, the older boys do have a role model in a male teacher. But the male teacher also has competition from the older boys—competition for the respect of the girls present. Tragically, there are male teachers who do not see this temptation, and who consequently fail as teachers of the young men. They are not really teachers in a classroom filled with young men and women, but are more like a bull elk with a herd containing (for the present) some younger, weaker males. But the younger bulls are growing, and conflict is inevitable.

A boy who gives himself to his work, and studies the way he ought to, will often have challenging questions for the instructor. If the instructor is insecure, this is often seen (in the interests of "maintaining decorum") as a threat instead of a promise. The boys who are "good students," according to this kind of teacher, are boys who ask "will that be on the test?" kind of questions. And the boys who actually probe and question, the boys who are future leaders, are treated as a problem. After a while they just shut up, and count the days until graduation.

Institutions will often have a rule that says, in effect, that physical force is never required. The dictum is that it takes a real man to walk away from a fight. And, while this is frequently quite true, it is *not* universally true. There are times when a boy should fight, and the wisdom which recognizes this is rarely found within institutional walls.

There is also pressure in today's politically-correct environment to exclude white male leaders from the curriculum as role models from history. This pressure is by no means absent from Christian schools, and the administration of any school that wants to make a difference in the world, and which wants some future men among their alumni, must resolve to stand against this pressure.

The result of all this is that many future leaders spend their entire career in a school biding their time until they can get somewhere that offers them scope. They graduate, go out, make a name for themselves, and astonish everyone back at the *alma mater.* But the astonishment is not so much a measurement of the graduate turning things around after he left as it is a measurement of the institution's blind spot in the area of masculine promise. The boys are not so much "sleepers" as they are young men which the institution did not have the capacity to recognize as promising. Because Christian schools *frequently* do not recognize or understand masculine promise, they do not educate in terms of it. Because they do not educate in terms of it, we have to acknowledge that there have been multiple tragedies, tragedies of missed opportunities.

Boys and Homeschools

A potential pitfall awaits boys who are homeschooled as well. From the foregoing, it should be obvious that I want this chapter to serve up some equal-opportunity criticism, and I am not here weighing into the debate about classroom education and homeschool education. I am supportive of every form of Christian education which does the job well. I have seen young men who were educated wonderfully at home, and I have seen the same thing in schools. I have also seen spectacular failures coming from both settings.

In a fallen world, every situation presents temptations, and this includes both the classroom and the homeschool. And in this fallen world, the *process* of education, both in a classroom and at the kitchen table, provides a temptation to fail our future men. Before pursuing this, a further distinction is necessary.

There is an important difference between homeschooling as commitment and homeschooling as ideology. What I have to say below applies in no way to those committed homeschool parents who, recognizing the difficulties, want to educate both their sons and daughters at home. Their "recognition of the difficulties" is seen through their openness to legitimate concerns, absence of prickliness, willingness to structure their homeschool in a way which takes reasonable concerns into account, and so forth. Just as a school has to take certain steps to nurture masculinity, so every homeschool has to do the same. Because the circumstances are different, the steps they take will be different. But action is necessary in both situations. Recognizing that this is necessary, without defensiveness, is a sign of strength. An ideologue does not have that kind of strength, and so his only defense is defensiveness.

Some folks unfortunately have an ideological commitment to homeschooling which circles the wagons at the first sign of any kind of criticism of homeschooling in any form, for any home. What follows here, I am afraid, will be implicitly critical of this mentality. If "doing it at home" is thought to be *automatically* better than anywhere else, under any circumstances, then what follows will be nonsensical. But the concerns presented here are not hypothetical, and wise homeschoolers will not be at all threatened by it, but rather encouraged and helped.

A boy who is homeschooled all the way through is growing up in a domestic, feminine environment. His sisters are being educated in a setting for which they are constitutionally suited. A boy, on the other hand, after his stint as a little boy, has his eye on the world outside. He was created to serve God out there in the world, and his education should be equipping him for it. But past a certain point, his mother is not equipped to provide this for him. Wise homeschoolers address this through the fathers's involvement in the education, vocational apprenticeships outside the home, sports competition, and so forth. But if such steps are not taken, and the boy grows up a homeboy without any training on how to become a man, the results can be pretty tragic.

The home is, by definition, domestic. A boy who receives an education identical to that of his sisters will receive it very differently than they do. In this circumstance, one of two things frequently happens. A boy can finally rebel against this environment, or he can accommodate himself to it. Rebellion is seen when Mom requires a twelve-year-old boy to do his math, and he invites her to try and make him. Accommodation is seen when the boy grows to *like* this domestic environment, and drifts into effeminacy. If he simply "waits it out"—like his counterpart in that classroom not conducive to student masculinity—he may discover that the limitations of his domestic upbringing stay with him, and he is not as prepared for the outside as he would like. As with the school that does not pay attention to this, the tragedy is one of a missed opportunity.

Education is teleological; it is directed to the end for which God made us. Because God made us for different purposes, men and women should be educated *differently*. This does not mean that they cannot be educated by the same people, in the same room. But at the very least, if those who are instructing them have egalitarian assumptions, and they teach the boys and girls as though there were no difference between them, then they are asking for trouble. The trouble they are asking for is that of wrecking masculinity in boys. Sexually-integrated education, whether at home or in the classroom, must acquire the wisdom of biblical discrimination.

Friends

Friendships are a big part of growing up, and they play a big part with those who never get around to growing up. Consequently, it is right that every parent be *actively* concerned about their childrens' friendships. At the same time, as with so many things, the Scriptures give us more direction on the subject than we tend to think. An active concern without scriptural foundation for it really amounts to blind meddling. Many recognize that the Bible does tell us that friendship is morally important. "Be not deceived: evil communications corrupt good manners" (1 Cor. 15:33). At the same time, Scriptures teach us more than just the importance of moral friends.

The first consideration is the preconditions of friendship. Second in line would be the descriptions of godly friendship given in the Bible—what exactly should parents look for in friends for their children? And the last consideration is what should be done about these truths in common problem areas?

Scripture tells us that even a child is known by his actions (Prov. 20:11). A child is revealing his heart through his words and actions just as adults do. Jesus taught us that out of the abundance of the heart the mouth speaks. This does not begin to be true after a certain age—it is a truth which governs the behavior of all the neighborhood kids. At the same time, because children are young, they have not had as much time to express that character fully.

This means that the character of a family will frequently have to serve as an indicator of the character of the child. And when sin appears, as it will, a family of godly character will respond to the situation rightly. Fewer things are more difficult than sorting out a fracas among the neighborhood kids when some of the parents do not share a commitment to the authority of Scripture.

Good families are hard to find outside of good churches. Friendship and family are covenant realities, and it is hard for them to flourish outside a covenant community—a place where the Word is faithfully taught and the sacraments are carefully observed. Parents who care about their sons growing up faithfully should therefore place a high priority on finding a faithful, flourishing church—and if there is none, they should carefully consider finding a town to live in which does have one.

What kind of friend should parents want for their son? A child who is overly talkative or verbally belligerent should be avoided: "A froward man soweth strife: and a whisperer separateth chief friends" (Prov. 16:28). A boy who talks too much will eventually hurt existing friendships, and if he is going to do this, it is wise to keep that door closed: "He that covereth a transgression seeketh love; but he that repeateth a matter separateth very friends" (Prov. 17:9). Suppose your son suddenly starts coming home with stories about other kids in the neighborhood, stories he picked up from a new acquaintance. The nature of the stories, and the amount of them, and your son's susceptibility to them, may tell you a great deal about whether this new source of lots of information would be a suitable friend. If he is Bunyan's Talkative, give him a pass.

Someone who desperately "needs a friend" will rarely make a good friend. A friend is one who overflows, not one who sucks everyone dry around him: "A man that hath friends must shew himself friendly: and there is a friend that sticketh closer than a brother" (Prov. 18:24). Emotional demands are not the demands of a friend—even if they are made in the name of friendship. Parents should therefore take care that their sons are not drifting into a close relationship with someone who is emotionally manipulative. Suppose you ask your son why he has struck up a friendship with someone who is (in your judgment) emotionally manipulative. If he says that he "feels sorry for him," or "stuck," this is a good indication that the friendship is off on the wrong foot. This is *not* to say that your son should not minister to those who are hurting. It is just that such ministry is not the same thing as friendship.

Scripture also has a good deal to say about fair-weather friends. When your son has a new bike, or sled, he may find that others start crowding around. He suddenly becomes the man in demand: "Wealth maketh many friends; but the poor is separated from his neighbor" (Prov. 19:4). While Jesus said that the use of mammon to make friends *was* an effective evangelistic approach (Lk. 16:9), the technique is still risky: "Many will entreat the favour of the prince: and every man is a friend to him that giveth gifts. All the brethren of the poor do hate him: how much more do his friends go far from him? he pursueth them with words, yet they are wanting to him" (19:6-7). Such friendships frequently wind up in various financial tangles (Prov. 17:18). These tangles can be significant for older boys, and comparatively slight when they are younger, but the principles remain the same. The basic issues surrounding loans, bets, oaths, and so forth, are all operative in elementary school. What a seventeen-year-old should not do with his car a seven-year-old should not do with his bike—e.g., loan it to a new friend for the summer.

Friendships grow around common interests, but these interests can be sinful or spiritually unhealthy. In order for the friendship to be healthy, the focal point of the friendship, the point of common interest, needs to be healthy as well. "And the same day Pilate and Herod were made friends together: for before they were at enmity between themselves" (Lk. 23:12). If a son needs a friend, he can probably make a quick one around a common, obsessive interest in video games—but that does not make it a good idea. Sin can run in packs, and if a son is in the middle of such a pack, there is no comfort in it for the parents. Other common but potentially unhealthy interests could include certain tattooed rock groups, driving aimlessly downtown, hanging out, or surfing the web.

All this does not necessarily mean that every friend must be a Christian. The apostle Paul had some pagan friends: "And certain of the chief of Asia, *which were his friends*, sent unto him, desiring him that he would not adventure himself into the theatre" (Acts 19:31). And he also assumed that Christians at Corinth might get invited to dinner parties thrown by pagans (1 Cor. 10:27). But this needs to be carefully watched, to ensure that the son is not getting into a situation beyond his capacity to handle. The *standard* situation should be one of godly friends, for all the obvious reasons: "I am a companion of all them that fear thee, and of them that keep thy precepts" (Ps. 119:63). The moral tone of a son's companions has a great deal to do with whether that son is drifting toward destruction: "He that walketh with wise men shall be wise: but a companion of fools shall be destroyed" (Prov. 13:20).

This issue of non-Christian friends should be resolved by considering whether the nonbeliever is a refugee from a nonbelieving world or an evangelist for it. If he is not attracted to the faith as it is lived out in the family, then he is not a wise choice as a friend: "Whoso keepeth the law is a wise son: but he that is a companion of riotous men shameth his father" (Prov. 28:7).

Friendship is defined by willingness to sacrifice. Ultimate friendship is seen in the sacrifice of Christ for His people (Jn. 15:13-15). In lesser (but similar) ways, friends identify themselves as such to the world by their willingness to give, to sacrifice. This may *appear* to be case, but later compromise or treachery shows that it is not (Ps. 35:14). Nevertheless, parents should look for friends who do not appear to be on the take. At the same time, it should go without saying, they should be training *their* son to be the same way: "A friend loveth at all times, and a brother is born for adversity" (Prov. 17:17). A true companion is faithful even when affliction makes sacrifice necessary. When this friendship is given in a biblical way, the sacrifice does not dampen the joy: "Partly, whilst ye were made a gazingstock both by reproaches and afflictions; and partly, whilst *ye became companions* of them that were so used. For ye had compassion of me in my bonds, *and took joyfully* the spoiling of your goods, knowing in yourselves that ye have in heaven a better and an enduring substance" (Heb. 10:33-34). Paul found this kind of friend in Epaphroditus, a "brother, and companion in labour, and fellowsoldier" (Phil. 2:25). The apostle John was this kind of friend to the saints in Asia—"I John, who also am your brother, and *companion in tribulation*" (Rev. 1:9). A true friend loves at all times.

Parents should not want flatterers around their sons: "Faithful are the wounds of a friend; but the kisses of an enemy are deceitful" (Prov. 27:6). By contrast, a friend should be wise and bring wise counsel. Parents should want a friend to be wise when their son would be foolish, and their son to be wise when his friend would be foolish. If a friend is wise, and close, his help can be invaluable: "Ointment and perfume rejoice the heart: so doth the sweetness of a man's friend by hearty counsel. Thine own friend, and thy father's friend, forsake not; neither go into thy brother's house in the day of thy calamity: for better is a neighbor that is near than a brother far off" (Prov. 27:9-10). A friend who only talks your son *into* things is probably not that helpful. A good friend encourages in both directions—you should be pleased to hear that your son was going to make a foolish purchase at the sports equipment store, but his good friend talked him out of it.

A good friend will push and challenge. "Iron sharpeneth iron; so a man sharpeneth the countenance of his friend" (Prov. 27:17). In many situations, a good friend will motivate in ways that a young man's family has not been able to. This is not necessarily a failure on the part of the parents; part of the parents' job is to find such friends, friends who fill in the gaps. And the gaps are there, of necessity. At the same time, a friend should not be obnoxious, or push when it is not necessary or wanted: "He that blesseth his friend with a loud voice, rising early in the morning, it shall be counted a curse to him" (Prov. 27:14). Examples would be a string of unappreciated practical jokes, or a tendency to sarcastic needling which is always excused as "friendly teasing." A good friend should have at least some basic social skills.

Scripture describes friendship as a *noble* thing. When a young man loves purity in his heart, and speaks that way, he will have the king for a friend: "He that loveth pureness of heart, for the grace of his lips the king shall be his friend" (Prov. 22:11). Such a young man should be the kind of person you seek as a friend for your son. But in doing this, it is important to bring up the kind of boy who would be the kind of friend that this sort of friend would want for a friend.

And this brings us back to the issue of friendship with God. No true friendship is possible apart from friendship with God. And the ground of that friendship, following the example of Abraham, is faith. "And the scripture was fulfilled which saith, Abraham believed God, and it was imputed unto him for righteousness: and he was called the Friend of God" (Jas. 2:23). The opposite of this faith is friendship with the world: "Ye adulterers and adulteresses, know ye not that the friendship of the world is enmity with God? whosoever therefore will be a friend of the world is the enemy of God" (Jas. 4:4). Friendship is inescapable. It will either be friendship with the world through lust or friendship with God through faith.

Training a son in his friendships is another important way to prepare him for marriage. He will learn the meaning of true companionship in his friends, and he will grow to understand that his future wife will be given to him as a companion: "Yet ye say, Wherefore? Because the LORD hath been witness between thee and the wife of thy youth, against whom thou hast dealt treacherously: *yet is she thy companion*, and the wife of thy covenant" (Mal. 2:14). A young man who does not understand friendship is not learning how to be a husband. And this brings us to the difficult part of maintaining standards of friendship. If a son is taught carefully from the time he is little, he will not have a problem with these things. The problem comes with the parents of potential friends who for various reasons do not make the grade.

First are the problems which come with the neighborhood kids. Most Christian families do not live in a neighborhood where they are surrounded on every side with godly families teeming with godly kids. Too often, the neighborhood is filled with under-supervised latchkey kids, and when they discover a house where a mom is actually occupied with caring for the home, that home can become the point of congregation. Sometimes the parents of such children can resent the small amount of love and discipline this contact brings.

When this situation happens, requests will soon follow—"Can we come in? Can we have a drink?" Some of the requests will be reasonable and some will not be. Although no invitations were issued, while these kids are at your house, you have a real authority over them. You would not go over to their house to tell them what to do, but they have come to yours, and so a practical authority is there. The part of reasonable host should be played, and unreasonable or untimely requests should be turned away tenderly but directly.

For the regulars, a set of rules can be established. The rules should be simple and easy to follow—e.g., no bad words. When our children were little, neighbor kids were welcome to come play in our yard, but if there was one bad word, our kids made them go home. They could come back the next day if they wanted.

It is far better to have these children at your home than to have the reverse problem—your kids at theirs. At your house, you have authority and control over what is happening. If that control is threatened, then you can simply send everyone home.

The second kind of problem is more difficult. This is where another family in your church wants to get your kids together, but for various reasons you are uncomfortable with it. Perhaps it is their laxity in discipline, or carelessness in entertainment standards. For whatever reason, you have reason to believe that friendship between your kids and theirs will not be spiritually healthy for your kids. So what do you do?

The fear is that if you say *why* you do not wish to arrange a friendship between your kids, you will give offense. This is quite possible. At the same time, this is why we need to live together in covenant community. While you may not wish for your son to be friends with their son, at least you can play the role of a biblical friend to them—and this means telling them honestly where the difficulty lies. This may cause problems, but gracious honesty is still best. Perhaps they will listen, and you may be a great help to them. But if the problem is, for example, the fact that their kid lies all the time, you should not protect your children by lying to them about it.

Clearly parents have important authority in this area. As with other aspects of childrearing, the practical authority should be exercised a great deal when the children are young and more sparingly when they are older. But the authority is always there. Most wise authority will be exercised at the point when friendships are forming, and not afterwards. But of course, if an existing friendship proves spiritually harmful, parents should be willing to bring a friendship to an end. This should only be done after much prayer and consideration, and after other solutions have failed. A parental overreaction—"You can't spend any more time over at . . ."—to some piddling problem or other is killing ants with a baseball bat.

CHAPTER FIFTEEN

Fighting, Sports, and Competition

When should a boy fight? Obviously we can deal with the extremes first, and then spend our time on the questions which ordinarily vex us. On the one hand, everyone would praise a boy who fought off a kidnapper who was after his little sister. And on the other, we would all agree on the need for discipline for a boy who gets in a fist fight with his brother over the last potato chips. In life-threatening situations, go ahead and fight. And in petty situations, when the authorities who could adjudicate the dispute are just around the corner, a boy should not even think about fighting.

But we still need a theology of fist fighting for the gray areas. What is a boy to do when he is regularly confronted by a bully, and the authorities either will not or cannot do anything about it? What does he do when he sees someone getting unjustly beat up, with no hope of getting adult intervention in time?

Frames for Fighting

The Christian faith is not pacifistic. The prophets have certainly given us a glorious vision of eschatological pacifism—a time *will* come when spears are beaten into pruning hooks. A time will come when men will no longer study war. This is the end result of the gospel's fruitfulness in the world. But until the time when men will learn war no more, they must still learn it. And we must understand that *every* aspect of manhood should start in boyhood. This means that boys should learn when, where, and how to fight.

Jesus teaches us about the thoughts and attitudes that are prohibited under the scriptural prohibition of murder. When God prohibits something, we cannot hide our disobedience through clever appeals to the technicalities.

You have heard that it was said to those of old, "You shall not murder, and whoever murders will be in danger of the judgment." But I say to you that whoever is angry with his brother without a cause shall be in danger of the judgment. And whoever says to his brother, "Raca!" shall be in danger of the council. But whoever says, "You fool!" shall be in danger of hell fire. Therefore if you bring your gift to the altar, and there remember that your brother has something against you, leave your gift there before the altar, and go your way. First be reconciled to your brother, and then come and offer your gift. Agree with your adversary quickly, while you are on the way with him, lest your adversary deliver you to the judge, the judge hand you over to the officer, and you be thrown into prison. Assuredly, I say to you, you will by no means get out of there till you have paid the last penny. (Mt. 5:21–26)

Jesus is not teaching against the law given by God. As we know, the law of God has not been abrogated. The Lord is, however, teaching against traditional encrustations that had covered over and distorted the law. The Bible teaches that grace and law are found in the Old Testament, and grace and law are found in the New.

Now the problem Christ was addressing was what we might call hybrid law. The first part of the cited law is the Word of God. But it was combined with something else—human tradition—a tradition that negated the force of the law of God. Rarely will religionists make something up from scratch. They will frequently use the raw material of scriptural words and phrases as their starting point.

So the first issue for us is that of name-calling. Jesus points out the *attitudes* that fall under the divine prohibition of murder. Of course, the actual killing of someone unlawfully is prohibited. But much more is also prohibited. First is the problem of anger without a cause—the person who gets angry with his brother *idly* is in danger of judgment. This would include boys who fight for entertainment, or who fly off the handle at things which are no provocation at all.

Second is the name-calling proper. *Raca* is a word of Aramaic origin; it is a term of utter vilification. Use of it puts someone in danger of being brought before the Sanhedrin. "You fool" is also prohibited—the word *fool* here is *moros*. The use of this puts one in danger of hellfire.

In other words, the attitude of a boy (even if it remains an attitude that never gets beyond words) can cause his case to be appealed all the way up to the highest tribunal there is—the throne of God. And what will be discussed at that tribunal? Just the big picture? Not at all—"But I say to you that for *every idle word* men may speak, they will give account of it in the day of judgment" (Mt. 12:36).

This means that boys *must* be taught that they may never fight for light or trivial reasons, and they must not be motivated by a personal disdain that is evidenced in the desire to wound through name-calling. Christ has prohibited *worthless* anger; Scripture does not prohibit anger across the board. We see this in the example of our Lord (Mk. 3:5), the express command of Scripture (Eph. 4:26), and the prohibition of *ungodly* anger (Eph. 4:3). "Do not hasten in your spirit to be angry, for anger rests in the bosom of fools" (Eccl. 7:9).

A boy must also be taught that he may not fight unless the fight is consistent with his love for his enemies. This requirement shows us the heart of the Christian ethic *for individuals*. We err when we take the biblical requirements for individuals and apply them to states, and the requirements for states to individuals. We do not understand governments, and as a result we commonly do not understand the instructions given to us in the Bible. This accounts for

P. J. O'Rourke's great observation that numerous individuals want to save the planet, and no one wants to help Mom with the dishes. A fight is a public act and is far too important to waste on private grievances.

> You have heard that it was said, "An eye for an eye and a tooth for a tooth." But I tell you not to resist an evil person. . . . You have heard that it was said, "You shall love your neighbor and hate your enemy." But I say to you, love your enemies, bless those who curse you, do good to those who hate you, and pray for those who spitefully use you and persecute you, that you may be sons of your Father in heaven . . . Therefore you shall be perfect, just as your Father in heaven is perfect. (Mt. 5:38–48)

The attitude Christ requires is straightforward. He intends for us, as individuals, to offer love and blessing to our enemies. Note the context. Moses required "eye for eye," and so forth in order to put a stop to the taking of personal vengeance. Personal vengeance rapidly escalates into a "life for an eye, life for a tooth." In contrast to this, God required *strict* justice, and this was to be administered by a civil magistrate, or at least administered according to civil law. But by the time of Christ, this phrase was turned into an excuse to justify the *taking* of personal vengeance, and Christ assaults this mindset. He is teaching us that, among His followers, there is to be no spirit of personal retaliation. There must be none of it. So in this situation, not only was the law of God being disobeyed, it was actually being quoted to justify that disobedience.

Jesus gives a series of situations which illustrate the attitude or demeanor He requires. The situations vary, but the attitude must be constant. If the attitude is absent, then this kind of obedience is never possible. If the attitude is present, then the applications will be obvious. But such obvious applications will not be obvious if we do not know the Bible, and if we do not understand the distinction between individuals as such, and government—meaning in this case, deputized individuals.

Do not resist an evil person. There are times when we must do this. There are times when we must not (Mt. 23). *Turn the other cheek.* There are times when we must do this. There are times when we must not (Jn. 18:22–23). *Capitulate in lawsuits.* There are times when we must do this. There are times when we must not (Mt. 18:15–20). *Go the second mile.* There are times when we must do this. There are times when we must not (Acts 16:35–38). *Give and loan money.* There are times when we must do this. There are times when we must not (2 Thes. 3:10).

We are not to go one way or another based upon our personal whims. Rather, our attitude should be constant, and we should adapt our behavior according to whether or not we are individuals (who must turn the other cheek) or deputies of a duly-constituted authority (and as such an authority, required by God to fight). For example, a father should teach his son that he must never fight over his own interests—like picking a fight with another kid because he does not like the shape of his head. At the same time, the father should instruct the son that he is fully authorized to fight a bully when there is no other way to restrain him. In the second instance, the son is appointed—a deputy of his father.

Popular wisdom wants to set the law of God on its head. This is how "love your neighbor" acquired the additional "hate your enemy." But Jesus then gives a series of injunctions which are a sheer impossibility for anyone in the flesh. There can be no mistake about the personal demeanor required of Christians. If someone is an enemy, then we must love them. If someone curses us, then we must bless them. If someone hates us, then we must do good to them. If someone spitefully uses us and persecutes us, we must pray for them. These are things which a soldier can do toward the enemy he fights, and a policeman can do to the criminals he restrains. A boy needs to learn how to make the distinction.

We are to imitate our Father in all things. We are to treat everyone we know, and meet, lawfully from the heart. This is what our Father does—He pours out common blessings on the just and unjust alike. We are to do the same. If we were to find a wallet with money in it, it should make no difference whether the wallet belonged to a personal friend or enemy. This is our imitation of the Father's common grace.

However, there are other aspects of our lives which are to be imitations of the Father's redemptive love. For example, husbands are to love their wives as Christ loved the church—they are to bestow love upon their wives, and upon no others. This is a distinction which is easy for us to master in our own dealings with our friends, acquaintances, and enemies. We must pray that God grants us an understanding of how this reflects His dealings with His bride, and His enemies. When we fight, we are modeling the particularity of Christ's redemptive love. We fight against someone, and we fight for someone.

War at Play

What about *playing* at war? More than a few adults have been concerned about boys playing at war with stick guns and swords. But boys who play at war are training at something men are called to do. It is as honorable as a young girl mothering a baby doll. But just as we do not want the young girl abusing a doll, neither do we want young boys pretending to do evil in war. Among the essential things that boys must learn here are honor and restraint. They should only learn what they *need* to learn, and they should not learn that which they must reject later.

This means that a boy who is playing with a toy gun should be trained to *never* use it more freely simply because it is not real. A small boy who is playing war with his brothers should be pointing and blasting away with the best of them. But if a lady from church comes over to visit the young boy's mother, and is standing in the foyer, and the boy comes up and tries to blow her away, the young warrior's mother should haul him off to the bedroom to be tried for war crimes. The visitor was a civilian and noncombatant, and Mother should be schooled in the principles of just war theory, and she should enforce the rules.

Related to this subject, young boys should obviously be trained in the use of real firearms. They should be fanatics about gun safety, and the rules of gun safety should apply whether the gun is real or not. By this I mean that carelessness with toy guns breeds carelessness with the real thing. When boys are playing at war, the guns should be pointed as they are in a war. When they are not playing at war, but rather hanging around, they should be taught to treat their toy guns with respect and not to casually point one at one of the playmates just to go *bang*. The reason for all this is that such behavior is preparation for a high and noble calling.

Some of the same testosteronic issues are involved in sports. Athletic competition is really mock war, and young men learn many of the lessons they need in the context of disciplined athletic competition. The subject is a dangerous one. When a ball gets involved in anything, emotions easily run high. Some Christian parents get fired up on behalf of their Little Leaguers, while others get spiritually stressed out at the very thought of competition.

We should first consider the lawfulness of athletic competition itself. Once that is addressed, we can go on to evaluate how our children are to participate in sports, if they do.

The first question concerns the lawfulness of athletic competition—is it right or wrong in itself? We must never forget that the Bible alone determines the boundaries of sin. Not once in Scripture is there a hint that athletic competition should be considered as immoral or sinful. The Bible, and not the traditions of men, determines the definition of sin. We have no more ground for saying that athletics is sinful than we have for saying that blue curtains are sinful. The defender of athletics does not have to prove from Scripture that sports are lawful; he must simply show that Scripture does not prohibit it. If God had wanted His children to stay away from balls in motion, He would have said so. With this understood, we can then let the common athletic metaphors and similes of Scripture come to the argument in order to pile on.

> Do you not know that those who run in a race all run, but one receives the prize? Run in such a way that you may obtain it. And everyone who competes for the prize is temperate in all things. Now they do it to obtain a perishable crown, but we for an imperishable crown. Therefore I run thus: not with uncertainty. Thus I fight: not as one who beats the air. But I discipline my body and bring it into subjection, lest, when I have preached to others, I myself should become disqualified. (1 Cor. 9:24–27)

We are not told to attract nonbelievers to the faith the way a hooker attracts customers, or to exhibit the persistence of a serial murderer. Paul here obviously appeals to an ordinary and lawful part of human life in order to teach us about the Christian life. However, too many Christians assume that once the lawfulness of something has been established, then we are free to pursue that thing in just the same way that the world does. However, the world has enough money to place all kinds of hooks in the lawful bait. And they do.

Three obvious examples of this should come immediately to mind. The first would be the entire problem of athletic competition and the Lord's Day. Granted there is no problem with a game of catch in the backyard on Sunday. But the world of professional sports, elevated as it has been to mythic proportions, now has a religious *cultus* which is in direct conflict with the worship of God. Not every child becomes a professional athlete, but multitudes of them want to. As parents instruct their children, this is a very important point of instruction.

Second, another obvious problem is that we have somehow assumed that the interests of speed, or some other function of athletic performance, somehow set aside the requirements of propriety and modesty. In the ancient world, athletes competed naked, and in the modern world, in some events, they might as well be. Obviously, one question that comes to mind is, "Where is that girl's mother?" But we err if we think that modesty is only a feminine issue. Questions concerning the whereabouts of a young man's mother can also be asked. We can tell that "athletics" has become a false religion because it has begun to dictate norms of behavior which contradict what the Bible says. Christians are to be modest, and if that slows them down, tough.

Third, as Paul's use of sports imagery indicates, athletics are rich with didactic images. We should not be surprised that the world rushes to teach false doctrine through athletics. In many athletic programs, especially the "parks and rec" kind, egalitarianism is rampant. "Winning and losing are not important. What matters is that every child comes out of the game feeling good about himself." What should distress us all is that this kind of paganism is taken by many Christians as the "spiritual" and "nonthreatening" approach. It is quite true that a competitor should not care about winning more than he cares about glorifying God. But although it may sound crass, the point of playing a game is to win it—and this is how young men should be trained to glorify God. Winning isn't everything, but it is the point of the particular activity.

Another false doctrine is that of self-worship. Our recurring Olympics parade scores of interviewed athletes who have learned their catechism well. "I discovered that I could only get here by reaching down and believing in myself." To which the Christian should be able to respond, "Pish. And tosh."

Nothing is neutral. Parents are to instruct their children to live as believing Christians when they rise up, when they lie down, when they walk along the way. And certainly when they run the bases.

CHAPTER SIXTEEN

Girls and Sex

Girls cause a lot of trouble. If it weren't for girls, we would have no moms, and if there were no moms, we would have no boys—and boys cause a lot of trouble.

Seriously, a boy can seem to be developing into an almost rational creature, but then when girls come into the picture we see what might be called the catnip effect. One moment he is upright and strong, a most promising young man, and the next moment, after a glimpse of *her*, he is barging into furniture and barking at the moon. This chapter will focus on just two areas: the general subject of relationships with girls, and sexual temptation (with or without "real" girls present).

Respecting Women

A basic issue discussed earlier deserves repeating—boys must learn to treat girls and women *with honor and respect*. In dealing with the opposite sex, they should have a deep, abiding, and instinctive need to honor women. Such a need is the result of ongoing discipline, from a father whom they respect, which discipline requires them to extend that respect to their mothers and sisters. They should be doing this for a good ten years or so before they even know what sex is. Then, when sexual or romantic interests arise, they will be incorporated into this framework of respect. If boys are not trained in rendering this kind of global respect, then sexual temptations can take up residence in that part of the mind where respect is not being rendered.

A two-year-old boy should be taught to respect his baby sister *because she is a girl*. A five-year-old boy should be required to say "yes, ma'am" to his mother simply because she is a woman. Young boys need to be taught to stand when a woman enters the room. They should be taught to hold open doors for women. They should seat their mother at the dinner table. These are not arbitrary or random cultural practices which have no meaning. They are a constant daily reminder to males—whose lusts when unmortified always degrade women—that women must not be degraded, but rather honored. Manners are therefore a form of sexual discipleship; they are sexual discipline. A boy who has learned to honor women everywhere will have difficulty in despising one in the back seat of a car.

Boys must grow up to be the kind of men who will be honorable in bed with their wives. They cannot do this in particular if they are unfamiliar with honor generally. They cannot do this with one woman if they don't know what it is to honor women generally. The Bible tells us that marriage is *honorable*, and the bed is undefiled (Heb. 13:4). Paul says that in marriage men should possess their vessels in "sanctification and *honour*" (1 Thes. 4:4). The impulses to dishonor in sexual desire are strong—our earthly members tend toward sin, Paul tells us—and so we need constant rebukes and admonitions. The cultural discipline of honoring women is very important. It is no accident that feminists have succeeded in getting women treated "equally" with men, and now that women are no longer singled out for honor, the men around them just go with their lusts. The results have not been at all favorable for women. After decades of established feminism, the end result is that far more women, in their relationships with men, are treated like dirt.

It is good for a young man to be around girls. Boys who grow up with sisters have a real blessing, provided they are learning how to honor them. Refusal to teach boys to honor girls and women will certainly result in grief, but grief too late.

A young man with a sexual problem has a sexual problem. But a young girl with a sexual problem usually has a security problem. For various reasons, she did not receive enough *securing* love from her father, and she is out looking for it from other sources. These "other sources" are willing to provide some faux security, in exchange for a little action. Many young women fall into this category. They are *not* looking for sex; they are searching for love and security. They fall into sexual sin because they are deceived into thinking they are loved, and so they compromise.

Imaginative Snares

For young men, there are two basic sexual snares. The first involves sins of the heart and mind—lust, pornography, and masturbation—and the second involves flesh-and-blood girls. In Christian homes, the former is far more common than the latter, but both categories present very real temptations.

Christian parents (and particularly mothers) must recognize that the temptation to lust comes down to us from our father Adam, from our members which are on the earth (Col. 3:5). They do not originate with the world or with Hollywood. The world can and does *enflame* these lusts, but the world does not create them. Thus, a young boy who has been kept at home, far away from the corrupting influences of the world, will still discover, after thirteen years, right on schedule, perhaps to his dismay and perhaps to his delight, strong sexual corruptions within him. This will happen whether or not he is regenerate. These corruptions will act, as one Puritan put it, like a gibbering ape within his loins.

When Jesus applies the law of God to this area, He continues His pattern of addressing the heart. Obedience to the law is not a matter of external conformity; it is a question of heart loyalty. Put another way, the well-respected and pious tend to think about *sins*. The godly are constrained by the teaching of Christ to think about *sin*—the condition of sinfulness, the fountainhead of all sins.

You have heard that it was said to those of old, "You shall not commit adultery." But I say to you that whoever looks at a woman to lust for her has already committed adultery with her in his heart. If your right eye causes you to sin, pluck it out and cast it from you; for it is more profitable for you that one of your members perish, than for your whole body to be cast into hell. And if your right hand causes you to sin, cut it off and cast it from you; for it is more profitable for you that one of your members perish, than for your whole body to be cast into hell. (Mt. 5:27–30)

When sin has dominion, the problem is heart rebellion. Jesus applies the law of God in a way which "decent" people do not like. His application makes all men adulterers. His teaching is plain. We see this principle when Christ taught about money. "And He said to them, 'You are those who justify yourselves before men, but God knows your hearts. For what is highly esteemed among men is an abomination in the sight of God'" (Lk. 16:15). What a fearful thought! God knows the heart. And what does He see there? "For out of the heart proceed evil thoughts, murders, adulteries, fornications, thefts, false witness, blasphemies" (Mt. 15:19; cf. Mk. 7:21). The source of sins is sin. The source of sins is the human heart.

Christ does not just say in this passage that real adultery is a matter of the heart. He says that such inner adultery is of immense importance to the sinner. How important is it? Rather than fall under the judgment of God for sin, the sinner should prefer self-mutilation. If removing eyes and hands would remove sin, then sin is serious enough to do exactly that. Because the context of this passage is the teaching about adultery on one side and then divorce on the other, I believe that Christ is alluding to the fact that self-castration is to be preferred to the wrath of God. But the problem here is that such self-mutilation will not work to restrain sin. Neither will asceticism (Col. 2:23). But *if* it would, then such action would be preferable to the judgment.

What is the offending member? What brings a young man to sin in this way? What produces such sin? And what must therefore be cut off? The answer is that the offending member is the heart. A man must have a new heart, or he will die. The doctrine of regeneration must be straight in our minds, for a tremendous amount of mischief has resulted from confusion at this point. We are not born again because we have repented and believed. Rather, we have repented and believed because God has given us the new birth. If our old hearts were capable of repentance and belief, then we would not need new hearts. Rather, we would simply need to improve the old ones.

What does God promise through the prophet? "I will give you a new heart and put a new spirit within you; I will take the heart of stone out of your flesh and give you a heart of flesh" (Ezek. 36:26). Who will do this? The only One who can. Jesus calls His followers to a genuine submission to the law of God and Christ. Since we cannot, we must cry out for a new heart. If we are believers who have drifted into compromise, then we must confess our sin to Him. He is faithful and just to forgive. Our new hearts enable us to look to Him for all our righteousness. True purity is found only there, and this true purity is required of every teenaged boy.

But many Christian homes preserve the ethical standards of the Christian faith, while not teaching the underlying foundations of all morality. Lusts are not generally visible in such a home, but they *are* present in the young man's mind. But the home life which surrounds him does not reveal on the surface any of this internal commotion. His father does not keep *Penthouse* on the coffee table, and he is not encouraged by his mother to make sure his "friend" is on the pill. Everything is squeaky clean, or at least that is how it looks on the outside. But the young man knows how foul his *thinking* can get, and he knows what no one else in the family knows, which is how often he indulges lustful thoughts and masturbates. It is not long before he concludes that the Christian faith is not realistic, or that it *is* realistic if you are a saint, which, judging from his behavior last night, he knows he is not.

Consequently, the principal "facts of life" which a young man needs are not the plumbing lessons, although that is certainly helpful in its place. He does not need biology so much as ethics. He needs teaching from the Word of God on the nature of lust, and what the Bible says men and boys are to do about it.

This means that fathers must *assume* that a difficult sexual struggle is occurring in their sons' lives. (And if a sexual struggle is *not* occurring, then the potential problems are greater, not less.) Having made this assumption, a father must talk to his son and teach him. The teaching must consist of more than, "Yeah, I had this problem when I was your age too." The teaching must be grounded in the Word of God—what does the Bible teach about masturbation, lust, fantasy, and so forth?

A father should check in with his son and not wait for his son to ask. Further, he should check periodically and regularly. Every son needs guidance and accountability from his father in this area. Sometimes young Christian men form accountability groups with other young men, which is not nearly as good an idea as it might seem. In many cases, it might as well be called the swimmers-drowning-together club. Say there are six guys in the group—what you have is six bundles of testosterone with feet. Suppose at a meeting one of the young men confesses to having visited porn sites on the web and then masturbated during the last week. Then the other five guys say, "Oh." Maybe they even exhort him strongly. On the other hand, if the young man had asked his *father* to be his accountability group, he would have found his computer privileges promptly revoked. In other words, it would be a real accountability, and not a pseudo-accountability which allows young Christian men to talk about their sexual sins without consequences.

Living Snares

The second category of potential pitfalls is that of actual sexual immorality. Pastors soon learn not to be surprised at the sexual messes that people can create, and one important lesson from this is never to assume that "it" can't happen "here." The *here* in question might be this particular family, this particular church, this particular community, etc. But when it comes to sex, wherever people live, the combustible materials are always present.

The world is full of available girls, and this fact cannot be made to go away through wishful thinking, or limiting one's contacts to just professing Christians. Whether a young man has contact with non-Christian girls or not, the possibility of sexual immorality is a very real one. It is insufficient to say that "all is well" simply because everyone spends a lot of time at church. Parents are often negligent because they are diligent in watching for the wrong set of danger signs. The purity of sons ought to be a regular item of prayer. And as parents are diligently watching for answers to their prayers, and as they are on guard against that which would threaten the object of their prayers, they need to be mindful of certain common indicators of trouble.

One very common indicator comes under the heading of low entertainment standards. In both music and movies, if a son is a regular consumer of whatever the world dishes up, *then he is being seduced.* There is a very common conceit which holds that today's young people are media-savvy, street-smart, and generally hip. The reverse of this is the truth. Today's young people are usually poorly-educated and unable to make the simplest ethical distinctions. The vocabulary of today's average fourteen-year-old is less than half of what it was in the 1950's. And three of the current vocabulary words appear to be *cable, dude,* and *Xbox.* Rarely has a generation arisen which is so easily manipulated.

There is no way that young men can watch, and be entertained by, movies which include displays of nudity, steamy sex scenes, and so forth, without being aroused by them. A boy who tells his mother that he can "handle it" is using what astute theologians in former ages used to call "a lie." Scripture tells us that bad companions corrupt good morals, and the movies a young man watches have to be reckoned among his companions. If he watches vile movies, he is being catechized by raunchiness. As a man thinks in his heart, so is he. Though she may be on the screen, and not in "real life," the harlot of Proverbs is still leading him to death. Exposure to all this makes a young man think he is sophisticated simply because he has grown accustomed to his environment, but this does not mean that he is able to discern the true nature of his environment. Just because a man recognizes the wallpaper in the brothel does not make him discerning.

Marinated in this corrupt stew, this young man then finds himself in the company of a young girl who is emotionally needy. Her father has not surrounded her with covenantal security, which is why she is needy in the first place, and he does not protect her well, which is why she finds herself alone with a horny young man. Her needs are very different from his, but the differences only serve to grease the skids toward intercourse. When she was little, she needed strong male affection. Because she did not get enough of it from her father, she began to act in a way that would gain her male attention. This, from a seven-year-old girl, was a nuisance, and she found herself further ignored, brushed away, or disliked. This only served to make her more insecure. That is when she started climbing on the laps of visiting uncles and friends, but she knew on some level that they did not really like it, which made her more needy. And then a miracle happened—she developed her figure, became sexually attractive, and all of a sudden she was awash in male attention. But this attention was not from uncles, fathers, and grandfathers. Rather it was from ravenous boys, and you do not want your son among them.

Sometimes a well-meaning boy who does not know his own heart very well will think that he needs to be near this girl to be her "protector." He sees her emotional vulnerability and has a deep desire to protect her, which he might think is high altruism. He lets her pour out her troubles to him. He tries to "minister" to her. No doubt he means well on a conscious level but he is not yet wise enough to recognize all the sexual undercurrents. He thinks that he can be her protector when in fact he is the chief threat she needs protection against.

Parents should also watch out for another kind of girl, one who might be called vicariously needy. She herself is not a sexual temptation to boys—say, because she is plain or overweight—and so she lives out her emotional needs vicariously, trying to get other couples together. In effect, she becomes a procuress, whether she knows what she is doing or not. Because of her management skills, it becomes very easy for a young man to go over to "Suzy's house" for some class function or get together. Because the parents know that Suzy is not attractive to their son, they assume too much. What they don't know is that the class get together is actually a loose collection of couples, and there are bushes and empty cars in the neighborhood.

This is related to another problem, which is when a climate or culture of secrecy develops among young people. This can happen in a class at school, in the church youth group, or among a circle of friends. It is very easy for young people to believe that parents know far less (about the world and about their kids) than they actually do. This makes them think they must solve their problems within their own ranks, without involving the adults. If the adults were involved, they think, some kids would "get in trouble" but no problems would be solved. So they keep their problems within the group and allow a culture of sin to take root. Even the "good kids" know far more than they ought to know without talking to parents about it. A good barometer that shows parents that this is *not* happening would be lively, detailed, and thorough conversations around the dinner table, with everyone in the family working through all the things that happened to them that day.

Parents should also beware of a son who seeks out a lot of time away—either to be alone or away from the family. A son who keeps away from his family is not therefore keeping away from his lusts. *They* don't stay behind with the family when he goes to his room, to the computer, or out with his friends.

Sexual immorality among young people in covenant communities is *always* accompanied by lying. It should also be noted that the pattern of lying usually starts before the immorality does; it is the lying which sets up the situations which make the sin possible. Interestingly, the lying often shows a legalistic and technical concern for the "letter of the truth." A young man could tell his mother that he is saving himself for marriage. She hears that all is well. He meant that oral sex doesn't count as real sex, and that he is saving *something* for marriage. We see here again the impact that lowered entertainment standards has had—along with the general degradation of our culture generally. The average kid in high school today knows about things that in previous generations were reserved until the second year of medical school.

All this is serious business, but it should not obscure what is being done. The Christian faith does not say *no* to a young man's sexual urges just to be a killjoy. Rather, it is more like a mother telling her son that he cannot have a bag of chips half an hour before dinner—because it will ruin his dinner. She knows what has been prepared, and she does not want his impatience to wreck it. In the same way, sexual impatience causes a lot of problems in marriage. We say *no* to that which would diminish or destroy the joy and purity and honor of the marriage bed.

CHAPTER SEVENTEEN

Courtship and Betrothal

When it comes to courtship and marriage, a young man must be trained to play an "away game." Parents of daughters can establish the rules of engagement, and a young man must be prepared for the father of the young lady who catches his interest. If he is a wise father, he will want to know this suitor's sexual history—not lurid details, but enough to know whether or not this young man is likely to be a faithful husband to his daughter. But there is no telling if his future father-in-law will be a wise man. A son may have met a Christian girl from a non-Christian home, or she may be from what is a messed-up Christian home. When your son goes to her father to receive direction, he might not get any. One result of this is that the sexual purity of the couple is not protected. In situations like this, it would be a good idea for the son to seek out the counsel and advice of his own parents. This is done, not because they have authority over the situation, but rather because they are trying to make the best out of a bad situation. The thing is being jury-rigged to work, but it is not how a couple should normally come together.

Questions of Betrothal

Some recent advocates of betrothal have wanted to have a "stronger" system than courtship, and this has an effect on the oversight of sons as suitors. But betrothal—where a broken engagement would require a divorce—is not physically possible in a culture which does not recognize that status. Without social enforcement, betrothal is the same as engagement. A generation or two ago, when a man could still be sued for breach of promise, betrothal was still possible. Advocates of betrothal want to get back to this, and thus far I am with them. Engagement should be understood as something more than really serious dating. There *should* be social sanctions for breaking an engagement without cause.

But behind much of the talk about betrothal there appears to be a more substantive difference, and this concerns the authority of parents over sons with regard to marriage. Of course, a fundamental aspect of family government remains even when a son is grown, has taken a wife, and has established a household of his own. The ultimate sanction that family government has is that of disinheritance. Just as the church excommunicates, and the civil magistrate executes, so a family has the authority to disinherit. If a son deserts the faith, he ought to be disinherited. If he marries outside the covenant, i.e., he marries a non-Christian, he ought to be disinherited.

But suppose we are not in this situation at all. A son is wondering about whether to marry this godly Christian girl or that one. His father does not have the authority to step in and require him to marry one over the other. A man will *leave* his father and mother, cleave to his wife, and the two of them become one flesh.

Fathers who want to control the details of their sons marrying are, ironically, behaving in a way that will make a very poor husband out of any son who puts up with it. When a man marries, he is stepping into headship and responsibility. He cannot do this well if he has never done it before. If right up to the wedding his mother is cutting his meat for him, and his father is tying his shoes, don't look for *that* marriage to wind up in the hall of fame.

So a young man ought to follow the pattern of biblical courtship. But words by themselves protect nothing, and nowhere is this more evident than with words like courtship. Calling something by the right name is no protection. Living before God with a right heart is our only protection.

Unless wisdom governs, words are like proverbs in the mouth of a fool—like the legs of a crippled man (Prov. 26:7). So it doesn't matter if it is called courtship, biblical courtship, or covenantal dating. What matters is more intangible. Unless wisdom governs, as I am fond of saying, courtship means that six idiots are involved instead of two.

In dealing with mysteries, wisdom is essential, and a set of wooden rules is useless. The Bible teaches us here that the relationship between the sexes is a profound mystery. This is true from the very inception of interest all the way through the fiftieth wedding anniversary. Paul tells us this explicitly: "For this cause shall a man leave his father and mother, and shall be joined unto his wife, and they two shall be one flesh. *This is a great mystery*: but I speak concerning Christ and the church" (Eph. 5:31–32). Those who want the formation of this great mystery to be reduced to a simple check-off list want something that cannot be. For those who have no hands, wisdom has no handles.

In our postmodern setting, it is harder and harder for anything to be abnormal, including some of the stuff we Christians do. Consequently, certain practices which could be thought of as very conservative or traditional can still get their fifteen minutes of fame. But the attraction here is the same thing that appeals to devotees of retro fads, or to re-enactors. It is not principled action; it is not wisdom.

Seeking Principles

A young man who wants a wife needs to remember certain key principles as he approaches the whole matter. What are some of the essential principles? The first is that attitude is first. In the arrogance of youth, one of the things which potential suitors demand is "a checklist" so that *they* can be in control of the process. But an attitude of wise submission shows deference and humility to those in authority.

Secondly, maturity matters. The conservative Christian world is generally consistent in creating "marriage nerds." In the secular realm, "worldly wisdom" is certainly immoral, but is far more cautious about the responsibilities of marriage than Christians are. As a general rule—not in every instance—but as a general rule, marrying before adult maturity is very foolish.

Third is the principle that young men have to know their limitations. Like a twelve-year-old boy who believes he can compete in a basketball game with grown men, many young men think they have a high view of marriage when they only have a high view of themselves. But one of the most essential characteristics of a husband is one of the most difficult combinations for men to achieve—confident humility. This is very hard to find in young men, and in our midst, it is not yet abundant.

A fourth principle is that of preparation: if you were going to live in a foreign country, would you prepare? If you were going to become an astronaut, would you prepare? If you were going to become a concert pianist, would you prepare? And so how do your sons prepare for the mystery of marriage? Or are they just marking time until it "happens" to them?

In all this, parents of daughters must be prepared to exercise a judicious authority. Parents of sons must be prepared to give godly and restraining advice. Parents should be involved primarily with their wisdom in the forefront, and not with their emotional attachments in the forefront.

If he is humble and careful, a young man still needs to know what to look for. We live in a fallen world in which God works redemptively. This means that nothing can be *assumed* to be in submission to God. But it can be assumed to be in submission to Him *or not*. It must be one or the other. Consequently, we must consider all things as a blessing, *or a curse*, depending upon its relationship to the Word of God. "An excellent wife is the crown of her husband, but she who causes shame is like rottenness in his bones" (Prov. 12:4). Women are a wonder to have around. Or a horror.

Avoidable and Laudable Women

The Bible teaches young men that certain women are to be avoided. When women are disobedient, the dislocations in the lives around them are severe. Obviously, this includes a seductive woman—"This is the way of an adulterous woman: She eats and wipes her mouth, and says, 'I have done no wickedness'" (Prov. 30:20). The wisdom of God found in Scripture brings with it as no small blessing the fact that it preserves a man from a horrible pit (2:16; 6:24; 7:5). This horrible pit is the mouth of an immoral woman; those who are hated by God will fall there (22:14). This must be seen by obedient faith, because an immoral woman *looks* good (7:10) and *sounds* good (5:3), and promises to feel good. Nothing is accomplished by Christians denying the obvious. But the Bible teaches that when all is said and done, adultery is a form of suicide. "Whoever commits adultery with a woman lacks understanding; he who does so destroys his own soul" (6:32).

Also to be avoided are quarrelsome women—Proverbs has much to say about the clamor of foolish women (9:13). Better to live in the corner of an attic than to be around a contentious woman (21:9; 25:24). Better to be out in the desert than to be around a quarrelsome woman (21:19). To be in a house that leaks during a downpour is about the same (27:15). In short, the Bible teaches that mouthy women are a pain in the neck.

But the picture is not all negative. Scripture tells us about the great gift of noble women, and this is what a young man should look for. But at the same time, he should be striving to be the kind of man that this kind of woman would be willing to be seen in public with. As we have seen, a foolish woman is a destructive force. In contrast, what are the characteristics of the obedient woman?

A godly woman is a sexually superior woman—husbands are commanded to rejoice sexually with their wives (5:18); they are commanded to be enraptured (5:19). This is something the husband is commanded to do, and is able to do, but not alone. In other words, a biblical wife can outdo all the one-night-stands in the world. Information to the contrary is nothing more than lying propaganda.

A scriptural woman is an edifying woman—she *builds.* "The wise woman builds her house, but the foolish pulls it down with her hands" (14:1).

Third, she is a gift. A woman from God, a good wife, is a tangible sign of God's blessing (18:22). Put another way, a prudent wife is from the Lord (19:14). Thankfully, the Bible describes what she is like.

When we affirm the biblical role of women, we must take care at the same time to avoid overreaction. The biblical woman and the traditional woman are not necessarily identical. Of course, there will be many areas where we see the traditional woman as being closer to the biblical norm than the "modern woman." But we are not to make judgments by grading on a curve. For example, consider the ideal woman of Proverbs 31. Such a consideration is not altered at all through the recognition that a woman capable of *everything* in this chapter is a "superwoman," that is, a rare find. This is assumed in the chapter (31:10)—and it is this which makes the description so helpful as a pattern for imitation.

Consider her work. This passage denies that a woman's place is *in* the home. It affirms that her *priority* is the home. So what does she do? What is she like? Her husband delegates responsibility to her (31:11) and is not foolish in doing so (31:12); she is a weaver (31:13); she shops for food effectively over long distances (31:14); she cooks and provides food (31:15); she buys real estate (31:16); she starts a farm with her accumulated capital (31:16); she works hard and manufactures quality merchandise (31:17–19); she is involved in philanthropic work to the poor (31:20); she thinks ahead and clothes her family well (31:21); she makes things for herself and dresses herself well (31:22); she poses no threat to her husband; she does not overshadow him (31:23); she is a fabric and clothing wholesaler (31:24); she is a wise woman, and a teacher (31:26); she manages her household

(31:27), to the praise of her husband and children (31:28–29); and she fears God, placing no trust in fleeting vanity (31:30–31). In determining this, the young man will not be looking at a lifetime of accomplishment. We marry at the beginning of our lives, after all, not at the end of them. But for a glimpse of what she is likely to be capable of, he can do worse than considering the young woman's mother. A young woman will probably be significantly like her mother in the future. In a similar way, a young lady should consider her suitor's father. This (obviously) is not an infallible consideration, but it is a consideration. A husband does not teach his wife to be a wife; she should have learned most of the lessons before she met her future husband. And many of these lessons were taught by her mother. This means that her mother's qualifications to teach are relevant.

But even when all such things are taken into account, the final word on this to young men should not be, "Get one like that." Scripture teaches us to look to ourselves first. A young man should primarily want to be the kind of young man a young woman like this would want to marry.

CHAPTER EIGHTEEN

Contempt for the Cool

It is not possible to write a book about raising young men without addressing the ubiquitous Nike swoosh. At some point, somebody with advertising authority decided that a lot of valuable advertising space was being neglected—there were simply acres of empty space just sitting there on tee-shirts, shoes, ball caps, warm-up jackets, and so forth. And so then another somebody decided that they could get a warmhearted general public to fill up these extra spaces with various corporate insignia. But unlike billboard advertising, where the advertiser pays money to hawk his wares, our new form of most-cool-wear requires the one giving the advertising space to pay money to the company for the privilege of walking around decorated by them.

This is a widespread cultural nuisance, of course, and perfectly idiotic, but how is it a problem for parents?

Winded Christians

The problem involved in this relates to the broader problem of what constitutes "cool." Fashion and peer pressure have no doubt been a problem for as long as more than three teenagers have been alive at the same time. Fads and fashion are nothing new in the world. But the problem of consumerist cool really does introduce a new tangle in this old, old story.

For example, in the fifties, when something became hot, something on the order of hula hoops, everybody had to have one. And they had to have one because they had to be like "all the other kids." But snookered by our new consumerist culture, we now see that everybody has to have the latest hot thing in order to be *different*. In other words, in the old days you had to be like everyone else in order to be like everyone else. But this new generation coming up is media-savvy and street-smart-hip; they have to be like everybody else so that they can be different from everybody else. The old conformists at least knew what they were doing. The new conformists haven't a clue. They have been massaged into thinking they are striking a blow for individual liberty and freedom of choice whenever they ask for money to buy just what all the other nonconformists are buying.

In the old order, parents at least had a chance to shame their children whenever they were clamoring for the latest thing. "Why do you want to be just like everybody else?" But parents today have been outflanked. The child wants to conform because he wants to be his own person and needs to assert his own individuality. He cannot be asked, "Why do you want to be just like everybody else?" That is exactly the reason why he needs to buy Lone Cool Cola, and not that other *stooopid* kind.

This propaganda angle is taken by advertisers everywhere. We are instructed to be our own dog, and the way to do this is to buy a beer that millions of others are buying. We are told by Burger King that "Sometimes You Gotta Break the Rules." If they really wanted to break the rules, they would put the meat on top of the two buns. And then add the lettuce. From the cradle on, young people have heard little else from advertisers. Do this, along with millions of others, and you will find your individual self.

Any child who thinks that Nike sneakers cost over a hundred bucks because the technology of sneaker making is so advanced these days probably ought not to be allowed by his parents to get his driver's license. He'd be dangerous on the road. Well over half of that price is simply for the privilege of being cool—as measured and declared by the ubiquitous swoosh. Who wants to trot around with whatever ridiculous logo Pony is using nowadays? The forehead reddens to think of it, until next week. And by the way, the transitory nature of cool is highlighted by how out of date some of these examples have become since the time of the first edition of the book. The difficulty here is a very practical one and involves teaching children to think like Christians. Because this seductive whisper is everywhere, it is easy to pretend that it is really nowhere. But the very real pressure comes to bear—frequently—whenever a pragmatic mother tries to make a shopping choice that would save a goodly amount of money, but would leave the kids without the necessary designer label. The poor children can't be cool without Tommy Whosit emblazoned on their hindquarters. And—until next week—going to school in Adidas is simply unthinkable—gotta preserve that precious individuality through consuming cravenness!

How silly we are being is hard for us to see. We have to use a thought experiment to get outside the boundaries of our thoroughly commercialized times. Just try to imagine Jonathan Edwards in a Hard Rock Cafe/Boston polo shirt. Or Patrick Henry sporting a Garth Brooks commemorative concert tour shirt? And the evangelical catch-up artists, manufacturing their copycat Christian designer goods, have transcended all this secular silliness and clambered up into a veritable nirvana of pious imbecility. Pagans are bad; we are worse.

Of course biblical parents must refuse to be tyrannized by the demands and dictates of cool. But they must be prepared to do more than simply make contrary shopping choices. The Bible requires that parents instruct their children in the art of biblical thinking. This is an important topic for dinner table discussion. After all, do you really want them to have to say, at the end of their lives, that they lived and died at the turn of the millennium, and all they got was this lousy T-shirt?

Imagery of Clothes

As with everything else, we have to turn to the Bible to find direction. The imagery of clothes in the Bible can scarcely be overestimated. This strikes us as alien on two counts. First, our clothing styles are very different from other cultures, (which is nothing new), but secondly, we have adopted a notion of clothing which is entirely unscriptural and unnatural.

In Scripture, clothing is not considered to be a neutral or unimportant thing at all. "Bless the LORD, O my soul. O LORD my God, thou art very great; thou art clothed with honour and majesty. Who coverest thyself with light as with a garment" (Ps. 104:1–2).

We always should begin our thinking with God, and the Bible describes His clothing. In the Scriptures, God describes Himself in various kinds of clothing, vengeance and glory to take two examples. "For he put on righteousness as a breastplate, and an helmet of salvation upon his head; and he put on the garments of vengeance for clothing, and was clad with zeal as a cloke" (Is. 59:17; 63:2–3). "Who is this that cometh from Edom, with dyed garments from Bozrah? this that is glorious in his apparel, travelling in the greatness of his strength? I that speak in righteousness, mighty to save" (Is. 63:1).

God also clothes His world. This pattern descends to the lowest level, and so our first consideration is to the natural world. "I clothe the heavens with blackness, and I make sackcloth their covering" (Is. 50:3). Or consider the grass of the field. "Wherefore, if God so clothe the grass of the field, which today is, and tomorrow is cast into the oven, shall he not much more clothe you, O ye of little faith?" (Mt. 6:30; cf. Lk. 12:28). God also dresses out other aspects of the world (Prov. 30:4).

God clothes His elect. It is not too much to say that the entire doctrine of salvation can be presented, in scriptural language, in terms of clothing (Zech. 3:1-5). Sin, judgment, justification, and glorification are all presented to us under the metaphor of clothing. The need for salvation is first. One of the first indications of divine mercy we see in the Bible is shown through clothes (Gen. 3:21). Ongoing rebellion is pictured through clothing. "Therefore pride compasseth them about as a chain; violence covereth them as a garment" (Ps. 73:6). What it means to be put right with God is described this way: "I will greatly rejoice in the LORD, my soul shall be joyful in my God; for he hath clothed me with the garments of salvation, he hath covered me with the robe of righteousness, as a bridegroom decketh himself with ornaments, and as a bride adorneth herself with her jewels" (Is. 61:10). "I counsel thee to buy of me gold tried in the fire, that thou mayest be rich; and white raiment, that thou mayest be clothed, and that the shame of thy nakedness do not appear; and anoint thine eyes with eyesalve, that thou mayest see" (Rev. 3:18). Clothing imagery helps us understand salvation: "The night is far spent, the day is at hand: let us therefore cast off the works of darkness, and let us put on the armour of light. Let us walk honestly, as in the day; not in rioting and drunkenness, not in chambering and wantonness, not in strife and envying. But put ye on the Lord Jesus Christ, and make not provision for the flesh, to fulfil the lusts thereof" (Rom. 13:12–14; Col. 3:9; Eph. 4:22).

We therefore cannot say that clothes are a "neutral thing." And descending from the realm of symbolism and metaphor, we come to the world which makes symbols possible. We see prison clothes (2 Kgs. 25:29; Jer. 52:32), the clothes of a widow (Gen. 38:14, 19), clothes of captivity (Deut. 21:13), clothes for mourning (2 Sam. 14:2), clothes for repentance or dismay (Gen. 37:34; Est. 4:1; Ps. 69:11; Is. 37:1), clothes to show joy (Is. 3:22), clothes to indicate sex (Deut. 22:3, 5), clothes for fine occasions (Ruth 3:3; Ezek. 27:24; Gen 27:15), politics (Mt. 11:8), and work (Jn. 21:7; Jn. 13:4). Lepers would indicate their disease through torn clothes. "And the leper in whom the plague is, his clothes shall be rent, and his head bare, and he shall put a covering upon his upper lip, and shall cry, Unclean, unclean" (Lev. 13:45).

Given all this, how shall we then dress? Or, more to the point, how shall our sons dress? In most cases, the problem is one of thoughtlessness. In modern America, clothing is assumed to be value-free, and an opportunity for one to express his own individuality (as though *that* were a value-free statement), or achieve his own personal comfort (as though *that* were not a worldview).

The problem today is that of the "invisible" uniform, the invisible worldview. Very few have eyes to see it. Remember that we are after the principle, and not a dress code, woodenly applied. The principle here is that sons must be taught not to hunger for a source of authority other than the Word of God—which is precisely what the concept of *cool* is. The problem is not this piece of fabric or that one, but rather a question of the source of legitimacy— is it to be found in the whims of designers and teenaged consumers, or is it to be found in the wisdom resident in Scripture?

The Depths of Pop Culture

Pop culture surrounds our growing sons. And we *are* entirely surrounded—by the minions of pop culture—and we need to cultivate a more optimistic view of our opportunities. At least there should be no difficulty figuring out which direction to shoot.

As sons are instructed, there have to be some key principles to guide us through the particulars. First, unless we are talking about a violation of the Ten Commandments, we must not rush to judge any particular manifestation of pop culture as "a sin," as evil in itself. Literacy in pop culture, and enjoyment of various features of it, are no sin.

Secondly, when sin *is* laid at the doorstep of pop culture, we must not locate it in the wrong place. Sin has to do with the human will and the law of God—obedience or disobedience. It is not found in the paint, alcohol, syncopation, or baggy trousers. All of these things can be used in sinful ways, some more easily than others, but sin, when it exists, must always be located in the human heart. The earth is the Lord's and the fullness thereof.

Third, all human actions have a moral component *and direction*. Everything we do, all day long, is aiding or hindering us in our maturity in Christ. Nothing is neutral. So when we have said that something is "not a sin," this does *not* mean it is impossible to sin with that something. Some things, Scripture teaches, are not at all sin, like wealth, but it is still difficult to avoid sinning with it. And so it is easier for a camel to go through the eye of a needle than for a teenager to enter the kingdom of heaven listening to alternative whiney rock.

But because of an immature "all or nothing" mentality in the evangelical world, as soon as anything is pronounced not *inherently* sinful, everybody rushes off to splash about in their Christian liberty, about which more later. And this is why the evangelical world today is crowded out to the borders with the culturally retarded. Cultural issues are always maturity issues, and maturity issues are *not* amoral.

Ken Myers has helpfully affirmed the distinction of high culture, folk culture, and pop culture. In contrast to the first two categories, pop culture is a consumption item. Both high culture and folk culture are vehicles which can readily carry "the permanent things" across generations. Some aspects of pop culture might be retrofitted to be able to do this, but this would actually be a conversion into high or folk culture. Even still, the categories are not watertight. Jazz is a combination of folk and high culture, and the blues (today) are a folk enclave within pop culture. But pure pop culture, *sui generis*, according to its own advocates, is momentary, each element of which is designed for extinction after its fifteen minutes of fame. Most practitioners, remember Milli Vanilli now, appear to understand this and get off the stage with alacrity, fifteen minutes on the dot, while others, like Robert Plant and Keith Richards, keep hanging around for some reason.

Of course, sin and rebellion can be expressed in any of the three types of culture. High culture can express rebellion against God at a high level, but it is not the greatest threat to us, because when the *avant-garde* goes stupid, virtually no one else pays any serious attention. Rebellious culture is at its most dangerous when it is seductive, initially attractive, and this is why pop culture presents such a danger. A *Penthouse* model looks more like a real woman than does a fragmented Picasso, which is why she seduces more men. Rebellious high culture only presents a problem to really smart intellectualoids—the only ones in the world actually vulnerable to the really stupid idea, as modern architecture shows us. Pop culture, on the other hand, has enough of a connection to the immediate desires and lusts of everyman to present a much broader threat.

And yet another factor to consider is the question of meaning. We all understand that a particular audible sound might be an obscenity in one language and perfectly inoffensive in another. The sound is the same but the moral point varies. The issue is what it *means*—and it is in the meaning that we find the human intention to obey or disobey God. Hence the meaning is essential in discussions of whether anything is sinful or not.

Debates with Christians who embrace pop culture are frequently hamstrung by the tenacity with which they insist on discussing the audible sound only, and never the actual meaning of the word. Modern evangelicals have a clear eye this way; they have a true imitative genius. They can copy anything the world produces, down to slightest flourish or embellishment. Whether trafficking in guitar licks or designer logos, they can always ape the real thing with exactitude. The only thing they don't know is what it all means. Modern evangelicals are like a drunk Japanese businessman in a karaoke bar singing along with the Stones. In his own boozy way, he knows everything about the song except what it is about.

Say we are dealing with a young man who has dyed his hair purple. I am giving him counsel and I tell him (as I *would* tell him) that this was sinful. He would want me to look up "purple hair" in my concordance and show him where the Bible prohibits it. But this is as unreasonable as the demand to find a list of English obscenities in a Greek lexicon. The Bible condemns rebellion, and the purple hair *means* rebellion. If he agrees, he has admitted the sin. If he disagrees, then he is an empurpled ignoramus, as the Sex Pistols would readily tell him, were they here.

This means that as we deal with the various manifestations of pop culture, we must learn to closely follow the teaching of the apostle Paul. In the realm of *adiaphora*, things indifferent, all things are lawful (*in se*), but not all things are necessary (will this get our culture where we as Christians want it to go?). Christians who are concerned for cultural reformation therefore have to reject the lowest common denominator tendency which assumes that anything that is okay is therefore okay. It should be so easy.

Constant Immaturity

A constant diet of pop culture is only legitimate if you don't want to grow up. Put another way, pop items as such are frequently inoffensive. But in the phrase *pop culture*, the word *culture* entails a direction, a tendency. It is the duty of any who aspire to be thinking Christians to ask what that direction is. And the second question concerns whether we want to go there. Because pop culture represents a full-scale revolt against cultural maturity, our answer should be that of course we do not want to go there.

So then, on to particulars. Parents need to teach their kids to ask pointed questions about music and movies, clothing and jewelry, and whatever other cultural stampede anybody thinks up next. The questions should all revolve around the central question of what it actually *means*. And when we come to understand the foundational meaning of the latest feel-good movie, body piercing, rap music, and

shrink-wrapped Twinkies, we should not be surprised when
it all comes out with the same basic message—do what you
feel, and go with the flow. This is described in the Bible as
folly.

Contrary to all of this, the biblical imperative must be
the discipline of *thinking* like a Christian. Legalistic tra-
ditionalists do not mind if the kids don't think about pop
culture, as long as they abstain from it—ignorance and purity
together. Come out from among them, and be ye separate.
Don't think—just so long as you don't. Meantime, the kids
who stay neck-deep in pop culture are contaminated and
ignorant. But both sides share an ignorance of what is really
going on.

This critique is aimed at the direction of the whole en-
terprise, as well as at the pandering which necessarily results
from taking this direction. We want to point out which way
the wind is unmistakably blowing. But Christian defenders
of pop culture want to debate the whole on the basis of the
one or two pockets of calm air they have found. We say, for
example, that the rock *culture* is in high rebellion against
the God of heaven, and someone is sure to ask if Clapton's
"Tears in Heaven" is evil. Of course not, it is a lovely song,
and there is plenty of other good stuff here and there—
which we appreciate through common grace. But the wind
is still blowing in the same bad direction.

Pop culture is a disposable culture for those who agree
to consume it. But because cultures are meant to be hand-
ed down to subsequent generations, because cultures are
meant to be *preserved*, a consumable culture is really an
anti-culture. And this is where pop culture and rebellious
high-culture reveal their similarity. No one will hand down
the works of this century's rebellious high art and architecture because it is all so mud-fence ugly. And no one will
hand down pop culture as an inheritance either ("And to
my great-grandson William, I bequeath all my Spice Girls
CDs . . ."). Pop culture was all eaten at the time, and there

isn't any left, for which the gourmands of future generations will be most grateful. Of course production in pop culture can frequently be quite demanding, but the consumption of it rarely is. Take a series of examples in several different areas. The music of Bach is of course demanding to perform, but it also makes demands on the *listener*. This is why the undisciplined mind avoids such music; it invites thought, contemplation, discipline, lots of icky things. More than one rock guitarist is an impressive virtuoso, but the fingerboard display makes no real demands on the hearer, other than a willingness to be blown over. The listener to classical music is impressively engaged; the devotee of such rock music is left, with a ringing in his ears, right where he started.

Modern movie making is frequently the same way. It is an impressive cinematic undertaking, millions of dollars to make, and to what result? Countless slack jaws, with glassy stares just above those jaws, staring at the eye candy.

In music, dress, food, books, entertainment, the powers-that-be cater to the undisciplined who want to stay that way. *The central sin of pop culture is therefore a sin of omission.* It displaces true culture, it does not itself adequately perform the functions of a culture, and sinners in a fallen world need to have the functions of a culture performed. Pop culture is a culture which does not enculturate, a culture which does not discipline. It is therefore an oxymoronic culture. In a biblical culture, a man expects his great-grandchildren to read what he has read, sing what he has sung, listen to what he has listened to. In an evanescent culture, like the one that surrounds us, a man expects to have all his "cultural" experiences buried with him. In the year 2525, do you think anyone will have heard of that dumb song?

Because pop culture makes no generational demands, it is an abdicating culture which does not discipline positively. And what happens whenever sinners are flattered and fed grapes like this? Any culture which does not discipline culturally will soon turn to the only alternative, which is to give way to cultural corruption. Which is exactly what has happened.

Sons cannot reject the idea of the cool if they are in the grip of folly. There are only two possible meals here—Wsdom sets her table and Folly sets hers. And hunger for wisdom and hankering lust for folly look very different, both before and after the meal.

Wisdom and folly are therefore *moral* issues. Proverbs teaches clearly that the fear of the Lord is the very start of wisdom (Prov. 1:7; 9:10). Wisdom is clearly the gift of a gracious God. "For the Lord gives wisdom; from His mouth come knowledge and understanding; He stores up sound wisdom for the upright; He is a shield to those who walk uprightly" (Prov. 2:6–7). Wisdom and folly bring two inevitable results: "The wise shall inherit glory, but shame shall be the legacy of fools" (Prov. 3:35).

But if wisdom and folly are moral issues, then they are moral issues for young men as well as old. "Wisdom is the principal thing; therefore get wisdom. And in all your getting, get understanding" (Prov. 4:7). The one who is urged to *get* wisdom is a young man who does not yet have it. In all his getting—scholarships, promotions, houses, jobs, etc.—he must make sure that the one thing needful is not missing. *Get wisdom.*

Fighting Idols

Famous phrases have a way of falling into the nether regions of our minds. We think we know them because we have heard them so often, but we really do not. Rather than true scriptural knowledge, such phrases usually just lull us to sleep. This is certainly the case for the phrase "as for me and my house."

> Now therefore, fear the Lord, serve Him in sincerity and in truth, and put away the gods which your fathers served on the other side of the River and in Egypt. Serve the Lord! And if it seems evil to you to serve the Lord, choose for yourselves this day whom you will serve, whether the gods which your fathers served that were on the other side of the River, or the gods of the Amorites, in whose land you dwell. But as for me and my house, we will serve the Lord. (Josh. 24:14–15)

Joshua is speaking to the people at the covenant renewal at Shechem. We need to pay attention to the context of his exhortation, and the content of it. Many misunderstand covenant renewal because they misunderstand forgiveness of sin. God picks us up where we are and not where we should have been. The effects of sin are so profound and so pervasive that sinners who fall away from God's covenant can never find their own way back again. After two centuries of disobedience, our people cannot even gather up the pieces, much less reassemble them.

First, the context: Joshua has gathered the people and has reviewed for them the history of their nation, beginning with the idolatry of Abraham's people. He talks about the deliverance of Abraham and his family and goes over the redemption of the Israelite people from Egypt. He mentions how the Lord had cared for them in the wilderness, and how the Lord fought for them as they began the conquest of Canaan. This rehearsal of their history, including the times of their disobedience and sins, is the basis of his exhortation in verses 14–15. He charges them to put away their idols—two kinds of idols.

They are to put away the idols they had in Egypt, before the Lord redeemed them, brought them out, and established his covenant with them at Sinai. They were charged to put away the idols they had retained from their pre-Christian past.

But second, Joshua tells them to put away the idols their fathers served on the other side of the River—the Jordan. Notice that these gods were gods that came into Israel after their great redemption from Egypt. In short, both kinds of gods must be put away—gods on the other side of the antithesis, and gods of the compromised synthesis.

The content of his exhortation here is simple and brief. Fear the Lord. Serve the Lord. Fear and serve Him in sincerity and truth. Put away all other gods. Joshua then sets before the people a stirring example. He does not know what course others may take, but as for him, he will serve the Lord, *and his house with him*. This includes, wonderfully, fearfully, our sons.

Our culture swarms with little gods, like the frogs of Egypt. But the gods of Egypt do have the advantage of being relatively easy to identify. They are the gods of antithesis. The gods of synthesis, the gods of gray and off-white, the gods which sidle up next to you in order to whisper devotional encouragements to you, are something else. These lords of compromise, these gods of soft counsel, are dangerous. Because of them the modern church is languishing, and the church is languishing because the households in Israel must tear down some idols.

Our Idols

What are the gods beyond our river? There are many of these spiritual pests, but a few bear mention. First of these is another god under the name Jehovah. Aaron sought to have the people serve the Lord, while hoping the golden calf would not be too much of a distraction, and who knows, perhaps to some poor unlettered Israelite such a concrete representation of Jehovah might even provide some kind of spiritual help. This is a free country, and there is no legal restriction prohibiting you from calling that pathetic little idol in the mind "Jesus." No reason a tiny god cannot be called Jehovah, Lord of Hosts, God of Battles. Of course, having considered the attributes of such a god, one usually doesn't.

Another such god is the god of the republicans and democrats—the god of civic religion and prayer breakfasts. This god would have been happily served by a pragmatic pagan like Cicero. This is the god to whom some want to offer prayer in the government schools. Such prayers would not get past the little two-foot space right above the acoustic tiles in most classrooms, which is just fine, because that is where this god lives.

Another is the god of personal peace and prosperity. He is the god of savings accounts, pensions, and insurance plans. The apostle Paul says in Ephesians that greed is idolatry. We have heard, many times, the assurance that material blessings are consistent with Christianity. This is quite true, but we must never forget the potential this blessing has to consume devotion to Christ. This wonderful statement, "as for me and my house," is not an inspirational quote to be matted and framed. It is a decision which exhibits a repentance broad enough to include the whole house, and certainly broad enough to bring all the sons along.

If we want our house to serve the Lord, then the house must be built where the Lord requires.

> "Therefore whoever hears these sayings of Mine, and does them, I will liken him to a wise man who built his house on the rock: and the rain descended, the floods came, and the winds blew and beat on that house; and it did not fall, for it was founded on the rock. Now everyone who hears these sayings of Mine, and does not do them, will be like a foolish man who built his house on the sand: and the rain descended, the floods came, and the winds blew and beat on that house; and it fell. And great was its fall." And so it was, when Jesus had ended these sayings, that the people were astonished at His teaching, for He taught them as one having authority, and not as the scribes. (Mt. 7:24–29)

Christ concludes His great sermon with a warning. Doing what He says to do, the way He says to do it, is paramount. It seeking to obey Him, we must not lean on our own understanding of His Word (Prov. 3:5). We must come as utter supplicants.

This means we must note where the distinction is not. Both the wise man and the foolish work equally hard in building a house. But the more the fool does, the worse he is making it for himself when the day of disaster comes. The more he puts into his house, the more he will lose. The more he puts into his house, the greater the pile of debris after it falls.

When the investment is a poor one, the situation is not bettered through having a tremendous amount invested. Foolish investors are not applauded for their effort. We never say that *that* was a foolish investment, but at least it was an enormous amount.

Christ and Wisdom

Christ labels the difference between the men as being one of wisdom versus folly. Both men hear the Word. That does not distinguish them. As James says, the one who hears without doing deceives himself (Jas. 1:22). So the fact that someone is listening to the Word does not distinguish him as wise. The wise and the foolish both hear and listen to the Word. Neither does activity distinguish wisdom. As mentioned above, the fact that there is activity associated with hearing does not distinguish the hearer as wise. Both men are active—both build their house.

Jesus says that the fool hears this sermon of Christ and does not put it into practice. The wise man hears the sermon and does what Christ said to do, the way He said to do it.

The distinction is not revealed at the beginning. Before the divinely-appointed time, the foolish man can taunt the wise for being too finicky in his building. Think of all the money *he* saved on foundation material! Think of all that the other will lose. Trial and storm are the point of revelation. Before that point, we may not be able to tell the difference between the professing fool and the wise man.

The text says that the people were astonished, amazed, at the teaching of the Lord. The Lord, as a teacher fully obedient to the law of God, was able to speak with full authority. Lesser teachers, sinful men, have two options. One is a ministry for fools—the Word is taught, but there is no genuine, ongoing, obedience. The result is teaching like the scribes—no authority, no astonishment.

But in periods of reformation and revival, when the teachers are like the wise man described by Christ here, the result is a powerful impact on the saints of God in the preaching and teaching. This is why it is so important that the elders of the people be held to the scriptural standards. These standards in 1 Timothy and Titus emphasize character, not professionalism. The scribes were professionals— boring professionals.

So we have noted the example of Joshua, saying that he and his house will serve the Lord. And we have seen the Lord teach us that serving him means building on the foundation of radical obedience. How is this to be applied in bringing up boys?

> Rescue me and deliver me from the hand of foreigners, whose mouth speaks lying words, and whose right hand is a right hand of falsehood—*that our sons may be as plants grown up in their youth*; that our daughters may be as pillars, sculptured in palace style; that our barns may be full, supplying all kinds of produce; that our sheep may bring forth thousands and ten thousands in our fields; that our oxen may be well-laden; that there be no breaking in or going out; that there be no outcry in our streets. Happy are the people who are in such a state; happy are the people whose God is the Lord! (Ps. 144:11–15)

We must learn to ache for the blessing of God—on our sons, daughters, fields and storehouses. Learning to do this without self-centered greed is grace from God indeed.

Young boys must be prepared and young men must help their parents as they are prepared as well. Ultimately this means preparing for marriage. But young Christian men have a tendency to prepare by talking about what they will "require" of a wife. Rarely do men talk about how they ought to prepare themselves—in their study, in their work ethic, in their behavior. When they do talk about it, they talk a lot about how their wives will have to do this or that. When this is the case, young men should knock it off and grow up.

Young men must prepare for battle—remember that the orientation of the man is not the same as that of the woman (1 Cor. 11: 8–9). The young man not only must prepare for marriage, he must also prepare for the world outside marriage. This is a world at war. A common mistake made by young men is to see war only when the shooting starts, and not the result of the antithesis placed between the seed of the serpent and the seed of the woman at the very beginning.

So young men, prepare your minds for battle—as Peter put it, gird up the loins of your mind (1 Pet. 1:13).

> Behold, children are a heritage from the Lord, the fruit of the womb is a reward. Like arrows in the hand of a warrior, so are the children of one's youth. Happy is the man who has his quiver full of them; they shall not be ashamed, but shall speak with their enemies in the gate. (Ps. 127:3–5)

Boys are future men. Young men are future men. This means they are future husbands and future warriors. When they arrive at that point, the responsibilities they encounter must not come as a surprise to them.

Liberty and Marijuana

This appendix is a modification of a booklet I wrote entitled *One Toke Over the Line*. It is a particular application of some of the principles discussed in chapter nine on Christian liberty. For many Christian parents, these questions are not really an issue, and so the discussion was placed in an appendix. But the issue is a live one in many families, and so this section is made available here.

There are limits (obviously) to civil and ecclesiastical authority, but those limits are not established by the agitated desires of private spirits, particularly by the spirits of ignorant nineteen-year-old boys. With regard to civil disobedience, an individual may withstand the authorities only if he has warrant from the Word of God to do so, and does so in a way that is an honor to the gospel. If he does not, then he may not.

When unbelieving civil authorities legislate against the mere use of wine, for example, they are doing so *contrary* to the teaching of the Bible. If the magistrate prohibits the use of wine at a sabbath dinner of believers, he is clearly overreaching himself. This does not mean that he *must* be disregarded—that civil disobedience is necessarily required—but it does mean that the magistrate has set himself against the clear teaching of the Bible. That segment of the Christian church which happens to agree with this kind of prohibitionism is a very provincial portion of the church—American Christianity over the last century or so.

But when the magistrate outlaws the use of marijuana, he is not assaulting Scripture in the same way. This does not mean that the use of marijuana necessarily *ought* to be criminal, but merely notes the fact that it is criminal, and that those Christians who want to disregard this law not only have no Scripture with them, they also have Scripture against them. Let me make this point particularly clear. I want to argue that marijuana use is clearly sinful, but I am not debating at this point whether it should be criminal. That is a separate debate for another time. Nevertheless, whether we debate it or not, it is in fact criminal. This means that those who want to use marijuana anyway are resisting the law from their own *sinful* position. They therefore do not occupy the same moral high ground that Christ would have occupied had the wedding at Cana taken place during Prohibition and been raided by ATF agents.

This is why we must recognize the distinction between sins and crimes. Americans are naturally meddlesome and have a deep prohibitionist streak. If something is disapproved of, i.e., thought to be sinful, the next step taken is the assertion that "there oughta be a law." But whether it is right or not, this "all or nothing" mentality is also shared by many of those who think that smoking dope ought *not* to be a crime. The facile assumption is made by some who think that since it should not be a crime, then it must not be a sin either. This is too easy.

For those who take the Bible seriously, we should be able to see right away that not all sins should be crimes. But we should also be able to see plainly that many "non-crimes" are clearly sinful. For example, covetousness is clearly a sin, a violation of the tenth commandment. God says not to covet anything that belongs to our neighbor, but the magistrate is not competent to deal with covetousness.

So I am not arguing here one way or the other with regard to the criminalization of marijuana use. We can at least say the magistrate should punish that criminal behavior which frequently accompanies such drug use, and the debate over whether the use of marijuana in itself should be against civil law can be left for another time. But even if the civil government legalized it, which it might, sanctions should still remain. Because it is so clearly wrong, the two other governments established by God should provide sanctions for any such drug use. The family and the church can (and should) discipline for noncriminal sinful behavior. In arguing that marijuana use is sinful, then it is important to note what is meant by "marijuana use." The proposition being argued here is that it is sinful to ingest marijuana to any extent that alters the chemistry of the body and causes a physiological response of *any* magnitude. I am not arguing that there is any sin inherent in the marijuana plant, and I am told that it can be used in the making of fine ropes. I am not saying that it would be a sin to hold marijuana in the hand, or to sprinkle it over the top of one's head. I am not saying that it would be a sin to ingest marijuana in minuscule amounts, amounts that have no effect whatever.

Such distinctions are necessary because the sinful mind is legalistic and always wants to push boundaries. People take dope *for the effect*, and I am going to be arguing that it is a sin to seek this effect. It is a sin to seek the strong forms of it—getting loaded—and it is a sin to seek the mild forms of it—getting a pleasant, euphoric buzz. If it has done its work *as a drug*, then that work has been a sinful one.

In what follows, the observations are made on the basis of objective knowledge of marijuana use, and not on the basis of self-reports from drug users who want to recommend the drug. We know a great deal about marijuana—it is a destroyer—and the hard data we have cannot be waved off as establishment hysteria over reefer madness.

Because marijuana is a toxic drug, getting to the point of physiological response happens rapidly. Unlike wine, for example, marijuana has an immediate effect, within minutes. Two sips of wine tastes good. Two hits from a joint, and the process of intoxication has begun. The active ingredient in marijuana is THC (delta-9-tetrahydrocannabinol).

Over recent decades, THC potency has regularly increased. In the sixties, ordinary marijuana averaged one-half of one percent THC. Today the average is three percent, with some forms (sinsemilla) getting to an average of 7.5 percent.

The half-life of THC in the body is three to seven *days*. Contrast this with the half-life of alcohol, which is about an *hour*. Marijuana smokers frequently think that they do not have a problem with the drug because "they only smoke on weekends." But by the next weekend half the THC is still in the body and is still having an effect. Even after the high has worn off, THC continues to impair the body's ability to function. For a chronic user, it can take months before the THC is out of the system, and even then, permanent effects on the ability to think can be measured and observed.

THC has an effect on the nerve cells in the brain where memories are formed. This is not a datum seen only in the laboratory. Those who are acquainted with drug users recognize at once the problem of "the space cadet." Marijuana users frequently lose their motivation to work (which is the *last* thing a young man needs), their concern over their appearance, and their grasp of ethical standards. Obviously, heavy users will be more heavily affected, but to the extent that a user is affected at all, he is harmfully affected.

Now that we have set the stage, what does the Bible teach?

> Therefore let us not sleep, as do others; but let us watch *and be sober*. For they that sleep sleep in the night; and they that be drunken are drunken in the night. But let us, who are of the day, *be sober*, putting on the breastplate of faith and love; and for an helmet, the hope of salvation. (1 Thes. 5:6–8)

The word translated sober here is *nepho*, and it means to "be self-possessed under all circumstances." Being sober is utterly inconsistent with every form of mental and spiritual drunkenness. Someone who is affected to any extent by

marijuana is not sober in the sense that Paul uses that word.
Peter says the same thing, using the same word.

> Wherefore gird up the loins of your mind, *be sober*, and hope to the end for the grace that is to be
> brought unto you at the revelation of Jesus Christ.
> (1 Pet. 1:13)

It is very interesting that Peter couples this requirement
to be sober with the requirement to "gird up the loins of the
mind." This figure of speech is striking; girding up the loins
is gathering up the robes, preparing for action. The Christian mind is to be in training, preparing to think clearly and
with godly precision. A lack of sobriety, a lack of *nephos*, to
any extent, is completely inconsistent with this. Two drags
on a joint and *nephos* is impaired. The clear-mindedness
which is required is necessary for prayer. "But the end of
all things is at hand: *be ye therefore sober*, and watch unto
prayer" (1 Pet. 4:7).

A related word is *nephalios* and the mindset behind it is
required of Christian elders as they set an example for the
congregation. This word means to be "in control of one's
thought processes," and to be "sober-minded, to be well
composed in mind." "A bishop then must be blameless, the
husband of one wife, vigilant, *sober*, of good behaviour, given
to hospitality, apt to teach" (1 Tim. 3:2).

We know from the immediate context that the required
sobriety is consistent with the drinking of wine in moderation. Paul says in the next verse that the elder is not to be
given to wine. The use of wine in moderation is consistent with *nephos*. But nothing in what we know of marijuana makes it consistent with this biblical requirement.
To smoke marijuana to get *any* level of euphoria from it is
clearly a sin.

Reasoning by analogy, we can also see that drug use is
excluded because it is designed to bring about the one state—
brain fog—which is condemned as a lawless application of

alcohol. "And do not be drunk with wine, in which is dissipation; but be filled with the Spirit" (Eph. 5:18).

The objection is often made that this excludes getting drunk with *wine* and does not exclude getting a buzz from marijuana. This is a good illustration of the legalistic, hairsplitting mindset of those who are attached to their sin. We too often think that legalism, the drawing of unscriptural boundaries, is the province of the overly righteous. But legalism is a sinful frame of mind, and it does not disappear even in the midst of licentious behavior. Sinners love to catch at words—it all depends on what *is* is—and we need to realize what is going on when they do this. When someone says that Paul prohibits "drunkenness" and not "getting high," we have an example of this kind of catching at words. Paul also says not to get drunk with *wine*. Does that mean that gin is all right? Beer? Rubbing alcohol?

If a man gets drunk with *beer* regularly, and the church disciplines him, may they use Ephesians 5:18 as part of their basis for doing so? The only reasonable answer is *of course*. Paul says not to get drunk with wine because it is one example of dissipation. Anyone who thinks that wine is the only route to dissipation doesn't get around much. The word for *dissipation* here is *asotia*, referring to a life that is prodigal or dissolute. The word for drunk is *methusko*, which refers to intoxication. If a man smokes dope until he is face down on the carpet, he is disobeying Ephesians 5:18. How he got loaded is not the point. If he got there with gin, beer, wine, or dope, the problem is the same one. As we have already seen, marijuana has an intoxicating effect almost immediately. This intoxicated state is unlawful, however induced.

But suppose this is granted, but a further question is asked. What about the fellow who is not wiped out? He smokes marijuana but remains (at least in his own mind) fully functional. He grants that "drunkenness" is always wrong, but denies that marijuana *has* to produce "drunkenness." Why cannot cannabis provide an equivalent experience to wine gladdening the heart of man? We have to look at this argument carefully. We have seen that drunkenness is flatly prohibited by Scripture, but we have to recognize that other uses of alcohol are approved and encouraged throughout the Bible.

In order to do this, we must back up. According to the Bible, alcohol has at least five lawful scriptural uses. Let's look at each and see if there is a parallel to marijuana at that point. The last one we will consider is the "gladden the heart" argument.

The first use is sacramental. "And he took the cup, and gave thanks, and gave it to them, saying, Drink ye all of it; For this is my blood of the new testament, which is shed for many for the remission of sins. But I say unto you, I will not drink henceforth of this fruit of the vine, until that day when I drink it new with you in my Father's kingdom" (Mt. 26:27–29). From Genesis to Revelation, we have no scriptural warrant for the use of drugs in worship. While this is a feature of numerous unbelieving sects and cults, it has no part of biblical worship. God does require wine in the Lord's Supper, but He does not require any use of marijuana sacramentally.

Wine has medicinal value. "Drink no longer water, but use a little wine for thy stomach's sake and thine often infirmities" (1 Tim. 5:23). Here we have to say that marijuana *could* be scripturally lawful *if* it were being used in a genuinely medicinal way. With this said, at the same time, we have to say that the current political push to allow for the medicinal use of marijuana does have a hidden agenda behind it—the issue is not medicine, but rather the legalization and normalization of marijuana use. The current science indicates that the proposed medical value of marijuana is greatly overrated. It is being pushed as a medicine for non-medicinal reasons.

Then there is the aesthetic dimension. "And saith unto him, every man at the beginning doth set forth *good wine*; and when men have well drunk, then that which is worse: but thou hast kept the good wine until now" (Jn. 2:10). One wine might be selected because it would go well with the beef, and another chosen because it complemented the pasta. Marijuana goes well with (recalling Cheech and Chong) Oreos and mustard. We have no scriptural reference to drug use as an aesthetic gift, but we do have a scriptural acknowledgment of aesthetic standards with wine. "No man also having drunk old wine straightway desireth new: for he saith, The old is better" (Lk. 5:39).

We also drink in order to quench our thirst. "After this, Jesus knowing that all things were now accomplished, that the scripture might be fulfilled, saith, *I thirst*. Now there was set a vessel full of vinegar: and they filled a sponge with vinegar [cheap wine], and put it upon hyssop, and put it to his mouth. When Jesus therefore had received the vinegar, he said, It is finished: and he bowed his head, and gave up the ghost" (Jn. 19:28–30). We see here that wine satisfies a God-given desire, that of thirst. We have no scriptural reason to think that marijuana satisfies any such natural desire. On contrary, marijuana creates a number of additional desires.

At last, wine has a wonderful celebratory function. "He causeth the grass to grow for the cattle, and herb for the service of man: that he may bring forth food out of the earth; and wine that maketh glad the heart of man, and oil to make his face to shine, and bread which strengtheneth man's heart" (Ps. 104:15). When a Thanksgiving table is set, when the glazed rolls are brown, when the turkey is done, and the crystal glasses are filled with wonderful wines, there the hearts of believers are filled with gladness. But when a room is filled with sweet, sticky smoke, the hearts of those present are filled with nothing but self-deception. True celebration is a *discipline*, accompanied with hard work, planning, training, and the fruition of joy. The use of marijuana is a celebratory slide downward, indulged in by the lazy and self-indulgent.

But doesn't this passage say that God also gives herbs "for the service of man?" Yes, but drugs are not at all in view. The word is *eseb*, and refers to herbs, green plants, and grass. It is talking about plants that work on behalf of man, not plants that cause a man's mind to become blurry. The lesson here is to eat your vegetables and salads.

Of all these, the only *possible* lawful use for marijuana is the medicinal, and the use to which everyone puts marijuana is the one use which is denied to alcohol. In short, if someone was affected by alcohol the way they are affected within minutes of taking just a few hits, I would insist they have had too much to drink. Why? Because their mind has been noticeably blunted; they are no longer sober-minded; they have started visibly down the road of dissipation. This is admittedly a judgment call. In just a few pages, we will be consider the biblical necessity of such judgment calls.

One word in the New Testament related to drug use is *pharmakeia*. It is the word which in Galatians 5:20 is rendered as *sorcery* or *witchcraft*. In the first century, the use of "altered state of consciousness" drugs was clearly connected in various ways to the occult. In the ancient usage, *pharmakeia* is usually used to describe some occult practice, related to drug use—potions, drugs, and so forth. This means that the translation of *sorcery* in Galatians 5:20 is probably a good one. But even today, the connection between drug use and occult practices is not entirely severed.

But even when there is no occultism, this does not make the prohibition of *pharmakeia* irrelevant to the modern "secular" drug user. Ancient drug use was far more "religious" than modern drug use. But so was ancient prostitution. When Paul commands the Corinthians to stay away from prostitutes, contextually the problem he was attacking was prostitution mixed with idolatry. In other words, men who worshiped at the Temple of Aphrodite would do so by having sex with the prostitutes there. This mixture of sin categories does not keep us from seeing the pastoral relevance of 1 Corinthians 6:12–20 to a modern "secular" use of prostitutes. In other words, a modern man could not defend his night with a hooker by saying that she was not a priestess. In the same way, *pharmakeia* encompasses more than one sin. One of them is the use of drugs.

We may also reason in the other direction. If we were to describe modern pot smoking to an ancient Greek speaker, and we asked him what word would be used to describe this practice (with no occultism in sight), he would still answer *pharmakeia*. Thayers lists as his first definition as "the use or the administering of drugs." The second definition is *poisoning*, and the third *witchcraft*. Liddell and Scott do much the same. First, it is the use of "drugs, potions, spells." The second definition is *poisoning* or *witchcraft*. Vine says the word "primarily signified the use of medicine, drugs, spells; then, poisoning; then, sorcery."

With these things in mind, the warning that Paul gives after he has listed the works of the flesh should be sobering to those who want to smoke dope as part of their Christian liberty. He says that "they which do such things shall not inherit the kingdom of God" (6:21). An awful lot rides on this.

Discussions over marijuana frequently find themselves diverted into interesting but irrelevant sidepaths. One of the characteristics of sophomoric insight is the ability to make superficial connections where no genuine comparison exists. The purpose of this short section is simply to show why it isn't a longer one.

The first superficial comparison has already been addressed—the moderate drinking of wine, or other forms of alcohol, cannot be compared to the immediate intoxicating effects of marijuana. At the same time, it must be said that with some very potent forms of alcohol, the possibility of comparison does exist. Rubbing alcohol would be ingested only for the sake of immediate effect, and so a comparison could be made. But in the vast majority of cases, the two activities are not comparable.

Another superficial comparison can be made to the smoking of tobacco. Tobacco is a room-smell-altering substance, but it is not a *mind*-altering substance. There are very good reasons not to smoke cigarettes, but for the most part they are not the same reasons for avoiding marijuana. But because tobacco is on the fast track to being declared "a drug" by our federal masters, it is important for us to think biblically here as well.

Some pietists have maintained that all tobacco use is necessarily sinful. A mindless response to this is that no tobacco use is sinful. But this is clearly false. Tobacco can be sinful for various reasons, even though it is not automatically sinful. If a man smokes a pipe once a month, I would be hard-pressed to show from the Bible how he was sinning. But if he is addicted to a pack of Camels a day, then obvious issues of self-control come to mind. And the same thing goes for Starbucks.

But marijuana is a mind-altering drug; it affects perception and ability to think. With "drugs" like coffee and tobacco, and anything else we might think of, the issue is not the loss of reason, because these are not mind-altering agents. But they do affect the body, and so the issue *can be* the creation of bodily dependencies, and a consequent loss of joy. The body is hard enough to subdue (Rom. 6:12) without giving it bunch of extra dependencies. "All things are lawful for me, but all things are not helpful. All things are lawful for me, but I will not be brought under the power of any. Foods for the stomach and the stomach for foods, but God will destroy both it and them" (1 Cor. 6:12–13). "I will not be brought," Paul says, "under the power of *any*." So the use of tobacco can easily be a moral issue. It just isn't *this* moral issue.

Proverbs Was Written for Boys

This book is intended to help fathers and mothers instruct and prepare their sons for a godly manhood. It would be foolish to attempt this without paying some *concentrated* attention to the book of the Bible written to do much the same thing—Proverbs. As various topical concerns about boys were addressed earlier in this book, the citations from Proverbs were necessarily frequent. But snippets from Proverbs is not enough. The book as a whole needs to be seen as a treasury of instruction for parents of boys.

First, the book of Proverbs provides us with an example of what sort of instruction is necessary. The book as a whole is applicable to the writer's son, and many passages apply the teaching specifically to him. What does God say a son should be told?

One theme comes up again and again. A boy must learn to be *teachable*. A boy finds it natural and easy to assume that stubbornness is masculinity, and that a bonehead is the complete man. But contrary to this, receptivity to instruction from both parents establishes a boy on the path of masculine wisdom. "The fear of the LORD is the beginning of knowledge: but fools despise wisdom and instruction. *My son, hear the instruction* of thy father, and forsake not the law of thy mother" (Prov. 1:7–8).

This is not said once, near the beginning of the book. It is repeated regularly. This, incidentally, should be an encouragement to parents who feel they have to repeat themselves too much. They might assume that the need for repetition means that they have failed. It does not necessarily mean anything of the kind. What it means is that boys are tough ground that need a lot of plowing. "My son, *if thou wilt receive* my words, and hide my commandments with thee" (Prov. 2:1).

It comes up again in the next chapter. "*My son, forget not* my law; but let thine heart keep my commandments: For length of days, and long life, and peace, shall they add to thee" (3:1–2). The young man is told to keep wisdom and understanding constantly in front of his eyes. "*My son, let not them depart* from thine eyes: keep sound wisdom and discretion" (3:21).

He is told to listen, not only to his father, but to the generations before. A godly inheritance of wisdom should be passed down from father to son, and from father to son again. "*Hear*, ye children, *the instruction of a father*, and attend to know understanding. For I give you good doctrine, *forsake ye not my law*. For I was my father's son, tender and only beloved in the sight of my mother. He taught me also, and said unto me, Let thine heart retain my words: keep my commandments, and live" (4:1–3). The father has received good instruction, as he ought to have done, and he expects his son to do the same.

A few verses later, he says it again. "*Hear*, O my son, and *receive my sayings*; and the years of thy life shall be many" (4:10). And since his son was looking out the window, apparently with some kind of old covenant attention-deficit problem, just a few verses later, he says it once again. "*My son, attend to my words; incline thine ear unto my sayings*" (4:20).

But a son is like that infamous Harvard man—you can always tells a Harvard man, but you can't tell him much—and God requires a father (and a mother) to go over the same material patiently. "My son, *attend* unto my wisdom, and *bow thine ear* to my understanding" (5:1).

The reader may be getting tired of this. Sons certainly do. But the one thing they must not do is get tired of this.

This kind of patient, repetitive instruction is precious gold. "My son, *keep* thy father's commandment, and *forsake not* the law of thy mother: *Bind them* continually upon thine heart, and *tie them about thy neck*" (6:20–21). This kind of teaching is not a pain in the neck; it is a garland around the neck. An honest answer is like a kiss on the lips, and this kind of repetition is like getting kissed repeatedly. This young man is not being nagged; he is being taught and adorned with glory. "My son, *keep* my words, and *lay up* my commandments with thee. *Keep* my commandments, and *live*; and my law as *the apple of thine eye*. *Bind them* upon thy fingers, *write them* upon the table of thine heart" (7:1–3). This instruction is a treasure he should keep in his storehouse; it is food that nourishes him in life; it is precious to him, like the apple of his eye; the words are rings for his fingers; he writes them down on the tablets of his heart. If he is a wise son, he does not say, "Aww, Mom! Trying to give me *jewels* again?"

The point is indisputable. "A wise son *heareth* his father's instruction: but *a scorner heareth not* rebuke" (13:1). The flip side of this is that a wise son also refuses to hear corrupt instruction. "*Cease, my son, to hear* the instruction that causeth to err from the words of knowledge" (19:27).

If the book of Proverbs teaches anything to sons, it teaches them to *listen*. Sons are told to hear instruction, receive words, hide commandments, forget not parental law, keep wisdom and understanding in view, attend to words, receive sayings, incline ears to sayings, attend to wisdom, bow the ears to understanding, keep a father's commands, forsake not a mother's law, bind wise words to the heart, wear them as a necktie, guard them as the apple of the eye, wear them as rings on the fingers, and, generally, taking one thing with another, to shut up, sit down, and *listen*.

All this comes before the content of the instruction. The principle is that getting a son's attention is very important. It is not enough for parents to give wise counsel and advice on a host of subjects when the son is not listening.

The first subject in the curriculum is to be teaching a son to hear.

This does not mean the content is unimportant. The content of the teaching is of course essential, but there is no point in bouncing good teaching off a boy's forehead.

And this means a second element is related to the first. In order to get a son's attention it is necessary to discipline him. Boys are not born teachable, and godly discipline is resisted by them. They have to be taught about this process as well. "My son, despise not the chastening of the LORD; neither be weary of his correction: For whom the LORD loveth he correcteth; even as a father the son in whom he delighteth" (Prov. 3:11–12).

The discipline is not intended as a behaviorist exercise. The son is not simply learning to associate pain with a particular behavior. The correction is to enable a boy to receive instruction. Since a son must listen, and since sons are not born listening, it is important to bring in reinforcements. Notice the connection here between teachability and discipline. "Apply thine heart unto instruction, and thine ears to the words of knowledge. Withhold not correction from the child: for *if* thou beatest him with the rod, he shall not die. Thou shalt beat him with the rod, and shalt deliver his soul from hell. My son, if thine heart be wise, my heart shall rejoice, even mine. Yea, my reins shall rejoice, when thy lips speak right things" (23:12–16). The father listens to instruction, he disciplines his son with the rod, and the son listens to instruction.

A father who will not do this may be sentimental about it, but he still hates his son. "He that spareth his rod hateth his son: but he that loveth him chasteneth him betimes" (13:24). And this refusal to apply the rod to the son will mean that the son will become a rod in the hand of God to bring calamity to the father. "A foolish son *is* the calamity of his father: and the contentions of a wife are a continual dropping. . . . Chasten thy son while there is hope, and let not thy soul spare for his crying" (19:13,18). Neglect of this duty brings disaster, while fulfillment of it brings peace and delight. "Correct thy son, and he shall give thee rest; yea, he shall give delight unto thy soul" (29:17).

Now what happens when a son has been taught to listen? What should a father and mother *say* to him? The book of Proverbs is not silent here either.

The book has a lot to say to sons about women—the kind of women your mother warned you about.

> My son, attend unto my wisdom, and bow thine ear to my understanding: That thou mayest regard discretion, and that thy lips may keep knowledge. For the lips of a strange woman drop as an honeycomb, and her mouth is smoother than oil: But her end is bitter as wormwood, sharp as a two-edged sword. Her feet go down to death; her steps take hold on hell. (Prov. 5:1–5)

There are two elements of the instruction here. The first is that this kind of woman looks good and starts out as a lot of fun. The second element is that she is a bitter, dead-end disaster. Too often devout parents will try to deny the sweeter than honey, smoother than oil part of this. But the son has eyes in his head, and he knows that what they are telling him is false. He concludes that their warnings about the bad conclusion are also false.

Parents should also emphasize the omniscience of God, the God who sees every teenage boy standing in front of the magazine rack. "And why wilt thou, my son, be ravished with a strange woman, and embrace the bosom of a stranger? *For the ways of man are before the eyes of the LORD*, and he pondereth all his goings" (5:20–21).

A son who is disciplined, and who receives instruction, is protected from the loose woman.

> My son, keep my words, and lay up my commandments with thee. Keep my commandments, and live; and my law as the apple of thine eye. Bind them upon thy fingers, write them upon the table of thine heart.

Say unto wisdom, Thou art my sister; and call understanding thy kinswoman: *That they may keep thee
from the strange woman, from the stranger which flat-
tereth with her words.* (Prov. 7:1–5)

It is important for a son to go beyond a simple recognition that immorality is bad. He must be taught to be vigilant, and to guard himself against sexual ambush. "My son,
give me thine heart, and let thine eyes observe my ways. For
a whore is a deep ditch; and a strange woman is a narrow pit.
She also lieth in wait as for a prey, and increaseth the trans-
gressors among men" (23:26–28). As the mother of King
Lemuel said to him, "Give not thy strength unto women,
nor thy ways to that which destroyeth kings" (31:3). The
same thing should be taught to every son of the covenant.

Sons are also taught not to be stupid with money.

My son, if thou be surety for thy friend, if thou hast
stricken thy hand with a stranger, Thou art snared
with the words of thy mouth, thou art taken with
the words of thy mouth. Do this now, my son, and
deliver thyself, when thou art come into the hand of
thy friend; go, humble thyself, and make sure thy
friend. (Prov. 6:1–3)

It should be noted that the son is enticed into a bad business relationship by a friend, a peer. This is one who doesn't
have any better idea of what the world is like than he does.

Sons are also warned against meddling in revolution-
ary politics. "My son, fear thou the LORD and the king: and
meddle not with them that are given to change: For their
calamity shall rise suddenly; and who knoweth the ruin of
them both?" (24:21–22).

More necessary is the warning not to be a gluttonous
and lazy frat boy. This warning is worth repeating at length,
and shows again the importance of wise instruction on life
coupled with wise instruction on instruction.

Hear thou, my son, and be wise, and guide thine heart in the way. Be not among winebibbers; among riotous eaters of flesh: For the drunkard and the glutton shall come to poverty: and drowsiness shall clothe a man with rags. Hearken unto thy father that begat thee, and despise not thy mother when she is old. Buy the truth, and sell it not; also wisdom, and instruction, and understanding. The father of the righteous shall greatly rejoice: and he that begetteth a wise child shall have joy of him. Thy father and thy mother shall be glad, and she that bare thee shall rejoice. My son, give me thine heart, and let thine eyes observe my ways. (Prov. 23:19–26)

The appetites of young men are frequently ravenous. When this is not governed with wisdom, the result is shame. "Whoso keepeth the law is a wise son: but he that is a companion of riotous men shameth his father" (28:7). This is the same kind of warning that was pointedly given to King Lemuel (31:1–5). Being able to afford it is not the point. And staying away from such companions also protects a son from murder and thievery (1:10–15).

In short, wisdom in sons is a true glory. Folly is just as obvious, and is a fundamental grief. "A wise son maketh a glad father: but a foolish son is the heaviness of his mother" (10:1). Sons do a lot of good, or they do a lot of damage. They bring great grief or great gladness. "A wise son maketh a glad father: but a foolish man despiseth his mother" (15:20). And again, "A foolish son is a grief to his father, and bitterness to her that bare him" (17:25). When a son is wise, he enables his parents to answer any accusation in confidence. "My son, be wise, and make my heart glad, that I may answer him that reproacheth me" (27:11).

Sons need work. And they need work in the areas outlined by the wisdom of God. When we heed it and teach our sons to heed it, we come to understand the sweet nature of true wisdom.

My son, eat thou honey, because it is good; and the honeycomb, which is sweet to thy taste: So shall the knowledge of wisdom be unto thy soul: when thou hast found it, then there shall be a reward, and thy expectation shall not be cut off. (Prov. 24:13–14)

Acknowledgments

For the categories and some of the terminology that structure chapter one, I am greatly indebted to the study course called *The Five Aspects of Man*. The course is developed and taught by William and Barbara Mouser, who have done outstanding work here. I recommend this course highly. It is produced by the International Council for Gender Studies, P.O. Box 702, Waxahachie (yes, Waxahachie), TX 75168. 1–800–317–6958.

For some fascinating support and background for chapter twelve, Natali Miller's senior thesis *That Serpent of Old* (Moscow: New St. Andrews College, 2001) is wonderful.

My thinking throughout this book has been greatly aided, prompted, guided, inspired, and rebuked by the following books:

Douglas, Ann. *The Feminization of American Culture.* New York: Farrar, Strauss, and Giroux, 1998.

Gilder, George. *Men and Marriage.* Gretna: Pelican Publ. Co., 1992.

Lewis, C. S. *The Four Loves.* Fort Washington: Harvest Books, 1971.

Mouser, William. *Five Aspects of Man.* Waxahachie: ICGS, 1998.

Podles, Leon. *The Church Impotent.* Dallas: Spence Publishing Co., 1999.

Index of Scripture

Genesis
1:26–28 — 14
1:28 — 29
2:15 — 15
2:18 — 31
3:1 — 102
3:14–15 — 15
3:15 — 37, 102
3:16 — 31
3:17–19 — 59
3:21 — 156
3:29 — 37
4:7 — 31
6:1-4 — 103
6:18 — 37
9:1 — 14
9:1–3 — 30
15:20 — 103
17:2 — 37
27:15 — 157
37:34 — 157
38:14, 19 — 157

Exodus
2:24–25 — 37
23:17 — 97

Leviticus
10:1–2 — 25
13:45 — 157
18:22 — 71

Numbers
12:3 — 49
13:33 — 103

32:23 — 53

Deuteronomy
1:4 — 104
4:46-47 — 104
7:25 — 71
12:30–32 — 25
18:12 — 71
21:13 — 157
22:3,5 — 157
29:7 — 104
31:4 — 104

Joshua
7:1 — 55
24:14–15 — 165, 166

Ruth
3:3 — 157

1 Samuel
15:22–23 — 25

2 Samuel
7:12–16 — 37
11:14–15 — 54
11:3–4 — 54
14:2 — 157
21:19-22 — 103

1 Kings
4:19 — 104

2 Kings
5:17–18 — 26

18:4 — 25
25:29 — 157

1 Chronicles
13:9-10 — 25
20:4-8 — 103

2 Chronicles
26:17–18 — 25
30:17–19 — 26

Nehemiah
8:1–3 — 97
9:22 — 104

Esther
4:1 — 157

Job
1:20–22 — 50
4:4 — 50

Psalms
8 — 30
22:27–28 — 51
35:14 — 120
38:12-13 — 50
69:11 — 157
73:6 — 157
74:13-14 — 103
102:28 — 12
104:1–2 — 156
104:15 — 81, 180
119:63 — 120
127:3–5 — 171

135:5-12 — 104
136:18-21 — 104
144:11–15 — 170
148:12–13 — 43

Proverbs
1:3 — 41
1:7 — 164
1:7–8 — 185
1–9 — 16
1:10–15 — 191
2:1 — 186
2:6–7 — 164
2:16 — 149
3:1–2 — 186
3:5 — 168
3:11–12 — 188
3:12 — 27
3:21 — 186
3:35 — 164
4:1–3 — 186
4:7 — 164
4:10 — 186
4:20 — 186
5:1 — 186
5:1–5 — 189
5:3 — 149
5:10 — 71
5:18 — 149
5:19 — 149
5:20–21 — 189
5:21 — 47
6:1–3 — 190
6:6–11 — 60, 62
6:20–21 — 187
6:24 — 149
6:26 — 71
6:32 — 149
7:1–3 — 187
7:1–5 — 190
7:5 — 149

7:10 — 149
8:18 — 67
8:21 — 67
9:10—164
9:13 — 149
9:16–18 — 65
10:1 — 28, 191
10:4–5 — 62
10:5 — 59
10:19 — 57
10:22 — 67
10:26 — 61, 63
11:4 — 68
11:18 — 71
11:24 — 67
11:25 — 67
12:4 — 148
12:15 — 56
12:24 — 65
12:27 — 62
13:1 — 187
13:4 — 60, 64
13:20 — 120
13:22 — 68
13:24 — 188
13:25 — 69
14:1 — 150
14:23 — 67
14:23–24 — 63
15:3 — 47
15:11 — 47
15:19 — 65
15:20 — 28, 191
15:26 — 47
16:1 — 48
16:4–5 — 48
16:7 — 48
16:9 — 48
16:11 — 64
16:28 — 118
16:33 — 47

17:4 — 57
17:9 — 118
17:17 — 121
17:18 — 119
17:25 — 191
17:27 — 57
18:2 — 57
18:8 — 57
18:13 — 39
18:22 — 150
18:24 — 118
19:4 — 119
19:10 — 69
19:11 — 50
19:13, 18 — 189
19:14 — 68, 150
19:15 — 64
19:17 — 68
19:21 — 48
19:24–25 — 62
19:27 — 187
20:4 — 63
20:10 — 71
20:11 — 117
20:13 — 70
20:17 — 64
20:23 — 71
20:24 — 49
20:29 — 41, 44
21:1 — 48
21:2 — 47
21:5–6 — 64
21:9 — 149
21:17 — 70
21:19 — 149
21:20 — 70
21:23 — 56
21:30 — 48
21:31 — 48
22:1 — 68
22:2 — 48

22:4 — 67
22:7 — 68
22:9 — 67
22:11 — 122
22:13 — 63
22:14 — 149
22:15 — 39
23:4 — 68
23:12–16 — 188
23:15–16 — 12, 35
23:17–21 — 69
23:19–26 — 191
23:24–25 — 29
23:26–28 — 190
24:13–14 — 192
24:21–22 — 190
24:30 — 62
25:14 — 72
25:24 — 149
26:6 — 25
26:7 — 63, 147
26:10 — 48
26:13–17 — 63
26:22 — 57
27:1–2 — 41, 71
27:6 — 121
27:9-10 — 121
27:11 — 191
27:14 — 122
27:15 — 149
27:17 — 121
28:6 — 68
28:7 — 120, 191
28:19–22 — 70
28:24 — 72
28:27 — 67
29:3 — 29, 71
29:13 — 48
29:17 — 189
29:20 — 57
30:4 — 156

30:20 — 149
31:1–5 — 191
31:3 — 190
31:10 — 150
31:11 — 150
31:12 — 150
31:13 — 150
31:14 — 150
31:15 — 150
31:16 — 150
31:17–19 — 150
31:20 — 150
31:21 — 150
31:22 — 150
31:23 — 150
31:24 — 150
31:26 — 150
31:27 — 151
31:28–29 — 151
31:29–30 — 35
31:30–31 — 151

Ecclesiastes
7:9 — 127

Isaiah
3:22 — 157
37:1 — 157
50:3 — 156
59:17 — 156
61:10 — 157
63:1 — 156
63:2–3 — 156

Jeremiah
6:11 — 44
52:32 — 157

Ezekiel
27:24 — 157
36:26 — 139

Hosea
6:7 — 36

Joel
2:16 — 96

Amos
2:9-10 — 103

Zechariah
3:1-5 — 156
9:16–17 — 43

Malachi
2:14 — 123

Matthew
5:21–26 — 126
5:27–30 — 138
5:38–48 — 128
6:12 — 50
6:30 — 156
7:24–29 — 168
11:8 — 157
11:29 — 49
12:4 — 26
12:36 — 127
15:19 — 138
18:15–20 — 129
21:28–32 — 96
23 — 129
26:27–29 — 179
28:18–20 — 14
28:19 — 51

Mark
3:5 — 127
7:21 — 138

Luke
1:74–75 — 80

5:39 — 180
11:21-22 — 103
12:1–3 — 54
12:28 — 156
16:15 — 138
16:9 — 119
19:6-7 — 119
23:12 — 119

John
2:10 — 179
11:51 — 26
13:4 — 157
15:13-15 — 120
18:22–23 — 129
19:28–30 — 180
21:7 — 157

Acts
16:35–38 — 129
19: 31 — 120
21:5 — 96

Romans
4:11 — 37
4:25 — 46
6:12 — 183
6:18 — 80
6:18-23 — 80
6:22 — 80
11:13–24 — 40
13:12–14 — 157
16:20 — 37

1 Corinthians
6:12–13 — 183
6:12–20 — 181
6:21 — 182
7:14 — 39
8:4 — 26

9:24–27 — 132
10:1–13 — 38
10:16 — 99
10:27 — 120
11:3 — 17
11:7 — 17
15:1–4 — 46
15:33 — 117

2 Corinthians
10:3–6 — 46

Galatians
3:26–27 — 99
5:13 — 79, 80
5:20 — 181
6:1 — 41
6:3 — 60
6:4–5 — 60

Ephesians
1:19–21 — 31
2:1–2 — 46
2:8–10 — 31
4:3 — 127
4:22 — 157
4:26 — 127
5:18 — 178
5:23–24 — 17
5:25 — 46
5:31–32 — 147
6:1–3 — 40, 96
6:2 — 42

Philippians
2:5 — 50
2:9–11 — 31
2:25 — 121
3:1 — 12
4:8 — 107

Colossians
2:20–23 — 25
2:23 — 139
3:20 — 96
3:5 — 137
3:9 — 157

1 Thessalonians
4:4 — 136
5:6–8 — 176

2 Thessalonians
3:10 — 129

1 Timothy
3:2 — 78, 177
3:7 — 78
5:23 — 179

Titus
2:6–8 — 44
2:14 — 25

Hebrews
2:5–8 — 31
4:13 — 53
5:14 — 78
8:6 — 38
9:15 — 38
10:33-34 — 121
12:2 — 31
12:5–6 — 28
12:25–29 — 51
13:4 — 136

James
1:22 — 169
1:24–25 — 64
2:23 — 122
4:4 — 122

1 Peter
  1:13 — 171, 177
  2:1–3 — 98
  2:15–16 — 79
  3:18–22 — 37
  3:22 — 31
  4:7 — 177

2 Peter
  2:19 — 80

1 John
  1:7 — 83
  3:6 — 78
  3:18 — 96

Revelation
  1:9 — 121
  3:16 — 25
  3:18 — 157
  20:2 — 102

Made in the USA
Middletown, DE
10 October 2022

12464020R00113